LESSONS OUT OF SCHOOL

Insights against a Backdrop of the Conflicts of the
Late Twentieth and Early Twenty-First Centuries

Nancy C. Russell

This book is a work of non-fiction. Unless otherwise noted, the author
and the publisher make no explicit guarantees as to the accuracy of
the information contained in this book and in some cases, names of
people and places have been altered to protect their privacy.

Archway Publishing books may be ordered
through booksellers or by contacting:

Archway Publishing
1663 Liberty Drive
Bloomington, IN 47403
www.archwaypublishing.com
844-669-3957

Because of the dynamic nature of the Internet, any web addresses or
links contained in this book may have changed since publication and
may no longer be valid. The views expressed in this work are solely those
of the author and do not necessarily reflect the views of the publisher,
and the publisher hereby disclaims any responsibility for them.

Any people depicted in stock imagery provided by Getty Images are
models, and such images are being used for illustrative purposes only.
Certain stock imagery © Getty Images.

Interior Image Credit: Jesseca Zollars-Smith

Scripture taken from the King James Version of the Bible.

ISBN: 978-1-6657-1799-1 (sc)
ISBN: 978-1-6657-1800-4 (e)

Library of Congress Control Number: 2022901483

Print information available on the last page.

Archway Publishing rev. date: 02/04/2022

Dedication

This book is dedicated to all who seek to understand and resolve the many conflicts arising within our human species, whether as parents, children, teachers, counselors, lawmakers, government officials, or health care researchers and providers.

Contents

Part 4: Eating, Drinking, and Breathing

Part 5: My Health and Theirs

Part 6: Basic Skills

Part 7: Lessons in Nature

Part 8: Glimpses into a Few Traditions

Part 9: Expanding Horizons

Preface

The writing of this book came about because of three dramatic memories from my childhood in Mount Vernon, a suburb of New York City. My life began in a relatively peaceful neighborhood, with the horror of World War II largely confined to the newspapers and radio news. This was before television, computers, cell phones, plastic bags, or plastic anything; before wrinkle-free clothes, hair conditioners, completion of the interstate highway system, or routine commercial air travel. These first three dramatic memories contained unexpected lessons, and once I had acknowledged those lessons as an adult, others quickly rose to the surface and became the lessons of this book.

I have benefitted from many years of formal education, in which I ultimately acquired a doctorate in public health (DrPH). However, the unexpected lessons in this book largely occurred outside my formal schooling. Some of these lessons, however, built on basic skills and knowledge acquired within formal schooling.

In the process of remembering these lessons, I have noticed that many arose out of pain and conflict either within myself or in the world around me. I am still living and reacting to life in the early part of the twenty-first century, which is roiling with conflicts. Perhaps some of my own observations and lessons can provide insights into the potential lessons of current and similar conflicts.

Each of these stories is independent of the others and do not need to be read sequentially. I suggest reading only one or two at a time, since reading more may simply cause you to become overwhelmed and confused.

Acknowledgments

I am grateful to my parents, brother, grandmother, adopted uncle, first husband and his family, our three children, my subsequent lover and companion of five years and his daughter, my second husband and his three children, and my many friends and teachers both in and out of schools. They have all contributed to the surprise lessons and adventures of my life. I would also like to thank my brother for advising me to simply spend a little time writing each day rather than waiting for a large piece of time. I thank my writing group in Wimberley, Texas, who provided me with valuable feedback. Finally, I thank the professionals at Archway Publishing for their detailed editing, valuable tools and advice.

Part One

IN THE BEGINNING

Chapter 1

AWAKENING TO LIFE

Pain filled the right side of my head and became more and more intense until suddenly it ended. I looked up to see my two parents and a third person, who said, "Her eardrum has burst, so it won't hurt anymore."

Oh! I briefly thought before I fell back to sleep. I was probably about two years old, and this was my first conscious thought. Recalling it now as I slowly learn other languages, I marvel at how I knew the third person was a doctor and understood the meaning of his words. It had apparently taken me a mere two years to obtain a working knowledge of English.

Beautiful, I thought as I reached for the light.

"Hot!" said my father as the light bulb burned my fingers and I screamed. What a lesson! Years later, I read the story of Icarus, who fell to earth after flying too close to the sun, which melted his wings. Later still, I recognized my own moments of great expansion and clarity only to be followed by the abrupt awakenings of reality back on earth. It has taken many decades to learn that, especially when influenced by drugs, alcohol, religion—or by simply letting my own thoughts run away with me, I had better check my perceptions against those of other people back on earth.

My playmates and I delighted in the juicy, sweet cherries we picked directly from the big, friendly tree we had climbed. Suddenly, we were marched inside a house, where a stern lady asked each of us which of our two hands had picked the cherries. I held out my right hand, and she slapped it so hard she made me cry. *How stupid*, I thought. *She thinks my hand did it all by itself.* Coincidentally my birthday comes at the beginning of July, when ripe cherries appear in the markets. I eat those "forbidden fruit" with gusto as I tell the child inside that we shall always appreciate cherries and their trees. However, we shall always be suspicious of those who don't want to share their fruit. That includes those who didn't want to share those apples in that ancient Garden of Eden.

How I wished I might meet the nice, motherly hen in my school reader. Perhaps I could even cuddle one of her fluffy, yellow chicks. But what chance did I have while living in a huge apartment complex of a big city? Then one day to my surprise, our day camp brought us all in a bus to the county fair. I wandered off by myself, looking for different kinds of farm animals. As I rounded the corner of a building, I suddenly felt a screaming mass of feathers and claws in my face. I screamed, threw up my hands, and fled in terror. In an instant,

I understood that I had stumbled upon a nesting hen and chicks. Why hadn't my schoolbooks warned me about that other side of a sweet mother hen—that protective and fierce side? The fierce side of any mother protecting her young or even of any woman protecting herself? I reflect on this early lesson every time a stranger in a grocery store calls me "sweetie." I think, *Beware of that other fierce side of me!*

My early awakenings weren't limited to unexpected pain; there were also joyful surprises. One day, as I walked along the street, holding my mother's hand, I suddenly had to pee. My mother took me through the next doorway into what she said was a movie theater. On the way to the restroom, my peripheral vision caught an amazing sight through some parted curtains. Many women with long, bare legs were dancing in a line—all kicking their legs high at the same time. *Oh,* I thought, *I have to do that.* And I did, many times over the years—ballet and tap dance lessons, ballroom dancing in gym class, and much later folk dances from around the world. Now in my eighties, I am a little slower, but I'm still dancing and loving it.

My early family consisted of three people: my mother (she), my father (he), and our dog, Oscar. One day, my father referred to our dog as "he."

"What?" I said. "Why did you call the dog 'he'?"

"Because he is a boy," said my father.

Hmm, I thought, *even animals are "he" and "she."* I understood then that I was part of the half that was female and never doubted it even later when I chafed at the restrictions placed on girls and women. I was a "tomboy," which meant

I liked to run and play like most of my friends and preferred trains and guns to dolls.

The movies of the 1940s and '50s were mainly westerns and war movies. Girls and women were portrayed as rather weak, silly, and not able to take care of themselves. Men, however, were portrayed as strong, heroic, and able to solve problems and take care of themselves. Accordingly, I strove to be like men—strong, smart, and capable. This, I thought, would make men like me, but strangely, this quality in me often seemed to threaten them. Anyway, a lot of that is in the past—or is it? Fortunately, I later learned of how we had all been misled concerning the strength, intelligence, and capability of women.

Further expansion of my perception in later decades has shown how limiting for both men and women to only think in terms of two rigid genders. How liberating it is, but understandably frightening, to allow ourselves to follow whatever skills and passions lie within our psyches without rigidly tying them to our genitals and hormones.

Chapter 2

MY PEOPLE AND THEIR PEOPLE

My earliest memories of other people began when I was about three years old. I was the child of an Irish-English Catholic father and a German-Scotch-Irish-Episcopalian mother. This background may not seem unusual now, but it was quite rare at that time. Both parents had white skin, as did the rest of our neighborhood, so I assumed this to be the normal color of all people.

One day I was surprised to see a man on the street with black skin. "Look," I said. "There is a black man!"

"Yes," my parents said, "people come in different colors."

How wonderful, I thought. I looked forward to seeing more people in different colors—red, orange, yellow, green, and blue. Sadly, I don't recall seeing anyone else who was black or any other color until a few years later, when we moved to another town. Even then, people with dark skin lived in a different part of town.

"What about television?" you ask.

"Television?" It hadn't yet become available. Even after black-and-white TV became available in the late 1950s, black people weren't shown other than as servants or primitive people, who lived far away in the almost-mythological continent of Africa. By then, my early delight and openness to differences had become buried beneath the fears and warnings of my family and other adults. Black people were associated with poverty, crime, and smelling bad. Personally, I never noticed any differences in smell, unless someone of any color had been sweating for some time. However, I did smell unpleasant odors on myself when I reached puberty or was sick.

My first real fears of other people, though, were of Germans and Japanese. Mind you, I had never knowingly met or even seen either of these people other than as our fearsome enemies of World War II in movies and news of the time. Strangely, I don't recall Italian people, our third enemy, being portrayed as quite as fearsome as the Germans or Japanese. Although my father didn't fight in World War II, he had fought in World War I, which also involved German people. I often heard remarks such as, "The Germans have always been warlike."

I participated in the patriotic parades of World War II following behind uniformed soldiers along with other children waving small American flags. I heard the nightly radio news and adult discussions of the rationing of food, clothing, shoes, tires, and gas. Frequently, those of us in the New York City area heard the chilling sounds of air-raid sirens warning that

German submarines (U-boats) or planes had been spotted off the East Coast. Those sounds warned everyone to turn off the lights. The brightly lit New York City skyline had previously silhouetted US ships at sea, making them easy targets for submarines. We could only use special candles, whose light was shielded by solid, black window shades.

My father was one of the volunteer air-raid wardens, who patrolled the streets to make sure no light shone out from any cracks. Once, according to my mother, our city neglected to turn off the streetlights. My father and his air-raid warden buddies, who were drinking in the local bar, decided they would all get guns and go around, shooting out the street-lights. Fortunately, a city worker was alerted and turned off the lights before this zealous band of drunks could further terrorize the neighborhood.

One day in the second grade, one of my best friends told me her big secret—her parents were German! Even though I was having nightmares about Nazi soldiers, I knew I had nothing to fear from either her or her parents and felt only sympathy. Many decades later at a high school reunion, I reminded her of that time, and she told me more about her family situation. She regretted never having learned to speak German because one day in New York City, her mother had spoken to her in German, and a man had yelled at her, "Don't you ever speak that language here! This is America!" The war ended in 1945 when I was in the second grade, but I had nightmares about fearsome Germans and cruel Japanese for decades to come.

The treaty ending World War II had barely been signed

when we learned about a new enemy—communists. This was very tricky since this group looked just like us, and some of them even were us. I then watched a new set of movies and TV dramas, in which equally scary people, mainly men, tortured people and shot those trying to escape. When I went to the dentist (a more immediate fear), I understood what it must be like to be tortured. That technologically primitive drill slowly ground away at my cavities, often without the numbing effects of Novocain. I tried to be brave as I remained silent while fantasizing about being tortured by communists, who soon joined the other monsters of my nightmares.

Against the backdrop of my fears of Germans, Japanese, and communists, I also learned that I should fear, distrust, and avoid black people, Asians, Italians, East Europeans, Puerto Ricans, and Jews. Imagine my surprise when I later learned that our own Irish ancestors had once been similarly discriminated against. My own mother had to break with custom to marry my third-generation Irish American Catholic father.

As if I didn't have enough people to avoid, I soon learned of an even larger group to distrust. When I was about eight years old, my mother explained that even though our family didn't have as much money as most of our neighbors, who could afford cars and televisions, we were of a higher "class" than they, who were merely "common."

"What does that mean?" I asked.

My mother continued, "We are not common because we know where we have come from."

"Oh," I remember saying, but all I knew was that my mother's family had come from Staten Island, New York, and before that from the states of Texas, Georgia, and Tennessee; and that my father's family had come from New York City and before that from Maine, Montreal, and Ireland. I asked whether my friends were also considered "common."

"Yes," she explained, "this includes your friends."

Can you imagine how confusing and depressing this news was? There was now an enormous wall between me and almost everyone else in the world. Years later, I faced down this teaching when I married someone, of whom my mother didn't approve. What was the basis for her disapproval? His family was part of that enormous group of commoners; that is, they were farmers. That's it; they weren't criminal, rude, poor, or illiterate. As I perceived them, they were educated, smart, interesting, friendly, hardworking, and prosperous.

When I look back, I regret that my childhood self wasn't smart enough to resist the prejudices of my family and neighborhood. Something did rescue me, though, from being entirely swallowed up in that confusing morass of fears … public schools. Although we lived in a white, Anglo-Saxon, and Protestant (WASP) neighborhood, we were on the edge of another neighborhood, which had a large Jewish residential area. When I began first grade, I was assigned to an elementary school in that other neighborhood, and there I had classmates who were about equally divided between Catholics, Protestants, and Jews.

One afternoon each week, those of us who were Catholic or Jewish were excused to go to separate religious instructions in our church or temple. During those sessions, I learned from the nuns that people who weren't Catholic would "go to hell" and that the "Jews killed Christ." I thought, *But this includes my mother, who is Episcopalian, and my friends, who are Protestant and Jewish and didn't kill anyone.* Even if their ancestors had "killed Christ," I couldn't understand why my friends of today should be held responsible for something that had happened almost two thousand years ago.

At home, I heard that Jewish people were too ambitious and "money grabbing." This mystified me, since all the adults I knew constantly talked about getting ahead and needing more money. Then one year, a Jewish company bought our apartment building, and we gained new neighbors who were Jewish. *Ah-ha*, I thought. *No wonder people seek money; it gives them rights.* I then valued getting to know these new people, who gave me the opportunity to babysit for their toddler, shared their classical music, and encouraged me to seek a college education.

Although I remained for a long time locked into a belief in Jesus as the Christ and part of God, I continued to have Jewish friends. One day in high school, a friend noted that I seemed to be spending a lot of time with a certain boy and that perhaps he was becoming my boyfriend.

"Oh no," I heard myself say, "he's Jewish." I felt instantly ashamed but also conflicted because Jesus as the Christ was a belief locked into my psyche. What a tragedy and missed opportunity that someone to whom I was obviously drawn should be relegated to the "other" category and out of bounds all because of someone from two thousand years ago, who was said to be the "Prince of Peace."

The more I learned about beliefs about God and Jesus

as the Christ, the more curious I became about what had happened historically and what the heck was going on now. Gradually I shed more and more layers of my "authoritative" Christian teachings and sought out other teachings in religion, science, and history. With each expansion of my universe of people, I lost more and more fears and became better able to focus on the true nature of individual people.

Although there were no black children in my public elementary school, I learned from my teachers about the cruelty of slavery and the freeing of the slaves after the Civil War. Reconstruction, however, was rarely mentioned; and when it was mentioned, it was often vaguely characterized as having been too extreme and even unfair to southern white people.

I felt ashamed that my mother's grandmother had lived on a plantation with slaves, and I wasn't reassured when I was told, "Of course, our ancestors treated their slaves well." Although I was inwardly skeptical of this, I was also embarrassed that I knew I had picked up some of my mother's feeling that merely having lived on a plantation somehow made my great-grandmother and family "important." My mother had also expressed the feeling that people in the southern states were more polite and friendlier than those in the northern states.

Shortly after hearing my mother's perspective on life in the south, I had an opportunity to hear the perspective of a descendant of slaves—not in my school but right in my own home. Our family life had suddenly been disrupted when my father was diagnosed with tuberculosis (TB) and admitted to a Veterans Administration hospital in another city. On the days when our mother visited him, she had to travel multiple bus lines, which meant a lost day for keeping up with the considerable housekeeping in those days of no automatic washers, dryers, dishwashers, microwaves, frozen foods, or wrinkle-resistant clothing. There was also the care of my brother, who was a toddler. She solved this challenge by hiring a woman to clean, iron, and care for my brother one day a week, and that woman was black.

There were about three different black women, who cleaned and cared for us during the next decade, and I particularly remember one woman with whom I could easily talk. One day I told her my mother had said that the southern states had people who were friendlier than in the northern states. She immediately responded, "I never want to be in the south ever again!"

Hmmm, I thought, *the same place experienced so differently by different people.* Over half a century later, we white people are once again hearing of different experiences by different people in the same places. Like most white people, I had learned as a child that I could always turn to the police for help. Yet, black children have had to learn just the opposite after two centuries of brutal mistreatment by white police.

In junior and then senior public high schools, I finally had classmates with skin colors that varied from white to cream to bronze to reddish to tan and black. Half a century before the United States elected a black president, our senior class elected a black president. Yet the minority of black students and majority of white students tended to sit at different lunch tables. Although our town had a sizeable population of black people, most of them went to the other high school, which was known as the technical school, while ours was known as the academic school. It was segregation by another name. During the civil rights protests of the 1960s, which mostly targeted buses, restaurants, and schools in the southern states, I often thought about the hypocrisy of northern states and cities segregating by other means.

I have lived most of my life in white neighborhoods and had mostly white friends, even in integrated schools in both the north and the southwest. However, in the late 1970s, I began working at a hospital where there were many people with black and tan skin. In the first few years, these seemed to be mainly black people from the south and brown people from Mexico, who worked with the cleaning and construction services. As the city of Houston grew, however, the entire workforce became more and more diverse and worked in different job classifications. I had many valuable opportunities to work with people of different colors, ethnicities, and countries. Most of them were hardworking, conscientious, and friendly; a few were irritable and cranky, just like the native-born white employees.

I observed the changing demographics of the hospital workforce over three decades. Particularly interesting were the weekly lunch-hour lectures known as "Grand Rounds," at which major scientific advances related to cancer were described. The lectures were interesting, but equally interesting were the changes I saw in the composition of the audience of about three hundred attendees. In the late 1970s, most attendees were white men, but by the late 1980s, this had gradually shifted to a more equal distribution of genders.

By the early 2000s, the ethnicity of the audience had dramatically changed to be almost entirely Chinese or at least Asian. I wondered what had happened. Had native-born whites stopped studying the biological sciences? Did the hospital have some reason to favor the hiring of Chinese people over others for its laboratories? In the year 2020, I chuckled when I learned the Trump administration had expelled the Chinese consulate in Houston for "stealing" scientific secrets. *Who do they think is doing most of the scientific work?* I wondered.

In 1981, I rented an apartment on the other side of the park bordering the Texas Medical Center. I was drawn to this area because I liked the idea of being able to ride to and from work through the park. The fact that I would be the only white person living in that apartment building just seemed to be a fitting test of my long-held beliefs in the equality of people. I told myself that I would just be experiencing what a black person might feel as the only one in an apartment in which everyone else was white. Naively, I imagined meeting neighbors who would be just like me in their political, religious, and other views. Although I did meet some friendly neighbors, most of my assumptions were rapidly overturned.

The first person I met was an obese woman, who was unemployed because of chronic back problems following years of lifting patients in nursing homes. She was receiving food stamps and welfare payments that were always late or otherwise inadequate. Being a vegetarian and a great believer in the sustaining value of peanut butter, I often shared it with her or just bought an extra jar for her along with various other foods. Even though I was an atheist, I was impressed that she sang in her church choir and looked like dynamite when dressed up and wearing special hats for Sunday morning services. On the other hand, it became somewhat annoying when she opened her door the instant I arrived home from work. I felt caught between the responsibilities I already had for my own life and those for someone else, who rightfully should have been receiving either adequate compensation for a work-related back injury or better training to avoid injuries or healthier food to avoid obesity or something.

Another neighbor owned a security company and expressed his good-natured chagrin when he learned more about me from his grandchildren, with whom I had been talking in the parking lot. One of my neighbors almost became a boyfriend. I say "almost" because he was much younger than I, and when I arrived by invitation at his birthday party, I received the most frozen, stony receptions imaginable from the other women at his party.

Things generally went well with my neighbors until the day I accepted my brother's offer of his stereo, which he was in the process of replacing. Although I had very much wanted to have stereo sound, an expensive item in those days, I hadn't wanted to bring in anything that would make me appear to be more prosperous than my neighbors. (Although I was probably more financially secure than my neighbors due to having a steady job, I had minimal savings, drove an older car, and didn't own a TV.) I initially resisted his offer but eventually weakened to the temptation.

Thus, I wasn't surprised when my stereo was stolen less than a week later. Although the burglary happened when I wasn't at home, it was my first experience of the fear aroused by having my personal space invaded. What really bothered me, though, was that my next-door neighbor indicated that the thief had been one of the other neighbors. Although burglary was common in Houston, knowing that it had come from a neighbor was too much. On the day I moved out, I met the new person moving into my apartment. We had a friendly conversation as he sat on the front step, cleaning his gun. *Ah-ha*, I thought. *That's how you do it; first, you let everyone know you have a gun.*

I subsequently lived in three other Houston neighborhoods, but I refused to buy a gun. Instead, I slept with my great-great-grandfather's Irish shillelagh club next to my bed. The last Houston home I lived in was in a mixed-ethnicity neighborhood, in which our home was broken into four different times until we finally had an alarm system installed. Each time had left my husband and me with an ugly feeling of having been personally invaded. When I consider this history of home invasions, I believe it wasn't the different colors or ethnicities of the neighborhoods. I believe it was the different economic status of individuals in or within driving distance of those neighborhoods. People without a steady source of income become desperate; a TV or a computer can be sold or pawned to buy a meal, gas, drugs, or whatever.

War and family fears of the "other" were deeply embedded

in my childhood mind and festered long into adulthood. At first there were nightmares about enemy soldiers; then there was horrible evening news of towns destroyed and children with burning flesh delivered by my own government. Such fears likely reside in the minds of many people and may even be passed on to later generations. In my own fleeting time of eighty some years, I've lived with news of World War II, the Cold War, the Korean War, more Cold War, nuclear threats, the war in Vietnam, the first Gulf War, the bombing of the World Trade Center, the Afghanistan War, the second Gulf (Iraq) War plus numerous "flare-ups," trade wars, and secretive prisons. Different enemies, different faces, different issues. Always living horror and always children and adults left behind with nightmares. It has taken four generations of my own family (great-grandmother, grandmother, mother, and finally my brother and me) to wrench ourselves out of the fears and biases of the US Civil War era. Other descendants of that war haven't yet lost those fears and biases.

Family fears of other people, recognition of the desperation of poverty, and fears of violence in my own and other neighborhoods have contributed to my nightmares. Such fears festering in anyone's mind can erupt in defensive reactions to real or imagined threats from those who look or sound different. In contrast, unquestioning trust in people who look like us can cloud our judgment, leaving us prey to con artists among politicians, salespeople, teachers, religious leaders, and would-be friends.

Wouldn't it be nice if we and our children and children's children could free ourselves from the horrid memories of past wars and avoid unnecessary current or future ones? Can we learn to perceive other people unblinded by their surface characteristics of skin, eyes, and hair? Can we learn to appreciate other cultures without fearing the loss of our own?

As one of the songs of the 1950s musical *South Pacific* proposed,

> You've got to be taught to hate and fear.
> You've got to be taught from year to year.
> It's got to be drummed in your dear little ear.
> You've got to be carefully taught.
>
> You've got to be taught to be afraid
> Of people whose eyes are oddly made
> And people whose skin Is a different shade.
> You've got to be carefully taught.[1]

Chapter 3

THE REMAINS OF GRAMATAN

Gramatan Avenue, the street on which I lived from the age of four through my high school years, had four lanes that ran from the traffic circle at the bottom of the hill through residential sections to a small shopping area at the top. From there, it proceeded over a highway, through another residential area, and northward into the town of Bronxville.

I was told that Gramatan was "some Indian chief," but that was about all anyone seemed to know. Today, with a bachelor's degree in history and access to the Internet, I figured that I could easily learn more about this person. A marker in the neighboring town of Bronxville stated, "Where In The Year 1666 Gramatan Chief of The Mohican Indians Signed The Deed Transferring Eastchester to The White Man".[2] Nothing further seems to be known about him as I could not find his name in any other major source such as "The History of Westchester County" or "Aboriginal Place Names of New York". Today he remains as much of a mystery to me as when I was as a child.

My family lived at 472 Gramatan Avenue, which was the largest building in the area, with five floors composed of 150 apartments divided into six sections. Built in 1901, it nevertheless had electricity, plumbing, gas stoves, steam heat in radiators, and dumbwaiters. Dumbwaiters—Yes, that was their actual name—were for hauling garbage from upper floors to the basement by pulling on a rope that ran over a pulley. These required manual strength to operate and were smelly from the spills and odors that had become embedded in the old wood. In place of refrigerators, we had ice boxes, for which large blocks of ice were delivered once or twice a week. One of the summertime joys for us children was to greet the ice man, who gave us large slivers of ice to suck. Another joy was hearing the bells of the truck that heralded the visit of the Good Humor Man. In those days, no one had a refrigerator capable of storing ice cream or much of anything for more than a few days.

An advantage of living in an apartment on the fifth floor was that we had a view all the way to the skyline of New York City on the horizon fifteen miles away. On the other hand, we had no insulation anywhere, with a flat tar roof directly over the ceiling of our apartment; it was cold in the winter and hot in the summer. During winter days, we had steam heat provided by a coal furnace in the basement, but it was turned off at ten p.m. and didn't start again until seven a.m.

I shivered as I huddled by the bedroom radiator I shared

with my younger brother. I dressed in the cold as I listened for the sounds of steam clanging in metal pipes far below. About the time the steam finally reached the radiator, it would be time to eat breakfast and rush off to school, to which I was often late. And yes, I really did walk a mile to school, often in snow, because our city didn't believe school children needed busses for such a short distance. In the summer, no one would dream of turning on an oven in those steamy apartments. Everyone ate salads, cold beef or chicken broth, sandwiches, and fruits; and then escaped outdoors, where the children played, the women chatted, and the men threw horseshoes or went to bars.

Although I envied the *normal* children in storybooks, who lived in single-family houses, I had much for which to be grateful. Our apartment wasn't jammed up next to any other buildings, and it had a large lawn, a huge sandlot for swings with a slide, and a large, vacant lot across the road. Most of my time after school was spent outside with about a dozen other children of my age-group.

Spring and summer were filled with games of hide-and-seek, hopscotch, tag, climbing trees, roller skating, riding bikes, bouncing balls, and jumping rope. In those days, jumping rope was what we would probably consider an Olympic sport today. It was fast and complex with jumps timed to intricate rhymes and rhythms. Sometimes there were even two girls jumping simultaneously between two turning ropes.

A special treat in the fall was to collect chestnuts from a huge tree. Unbeknownst to us was that this was one of the last surviving chestnut trees in North America. Another tree, known as "the triangle tree," was the beloved center for our games of tag and hide-and-seek. It was an old oak that had hung on for an unknown number of years. Most of its rotted core had been carved out and reinforced with iron bars. It was finally cut down, and we children felt the loss of an old friend.

We children spent winter sledding down the hill next to our apartment building, making snowmen, and digging snow tunnels. We played in heavy woolen snowsuits, which became wet around the wrists and gave us rashes, but we loved it. How wonderful that today's children and adults can enjoy winter sports in lightweight, insulated clothing—even if it is synthetic and provides environmental challenges when it finally breaks down.

During World War II, the government distributed free seeds to students in schools and encouraged residents to plant "Victory Gardens". (Recently I read that US victory gardens were responsible for 40 percent of domestic food supplies during that war.) Our apartment building was next to a large vacant lot which our parents used for victory gardens. We children then used the weed filled spaces between the gardens as favorite places for hiding and building forts which were also undoubtedly responsible for our insect bites and poison ivy.

The less obvious feature of that lot was that it was a "no-man's-land" between ours and the adjoining neighborhood. Our neighborhood was largely inhabited north European immigrants from previous generations while the other neighborhood was largely inhabited by more recent Italian immigrants. One of my dim memories is one of which I'm not proud. Every so often one of us kids would yell, "Let's go have a rock fight with the Italians!" About a dozen of us then grabbed rocks and ran across the road into the field, yelling. We then saw a similar group running toward us and yelling from the opposite side. Both sides hurled rocks at each other, then screamed and ran home.

Amazingly, I don't recall anyone ever getting hurt in these fights, but why were we doing them? Were we following through on the prejudices of our parents or war movies or cowboy-Indian movies, or were we simply being mischievous children, looking for excitement? In recent decades, I have seen children on TV who live in war zones, throw rocks at occupying soldiers or border guards, which is understandable. We, however, weren't in a war zone and had never been threatened or hurt by any Italians; we didn't even know any Italians.

The real war in Europe seemed far away at that time, but not so long ago our own neighborhood had been part of a war zone. A mere three hundred years before our time, all Westchester County, Manhattan Island, and parts of Connecticut had experienced decades of struggle in the early 1600s between the Dutch, the English, and the native tribes. A story still circulating in my childhood was the murder in 1643 of all but one of the family of Anne Hutchinson, a refugee from Connecticut where she had been accused of witchcraft. This killing itself was said to have been a reprisal for a previous attack by the Dutch governor's troops on Siwanoy refugees. Another widespread massacre of settlers was said to have been revenge for the killing by Dutch troops of an Indian woman who had stolen a peach.

Unexpectedly, my further reading of the history of Westchester County indicated no further battles between the Native Americans, Dutch and English. According to the "History of Westchester County, Volume I", further land acquisitions were accomplished through reciprocal exchanges of goods for parcels of land in Westchester. The Dutch and English who purchased the land, however, largely used it for agriculture and by 1720, most of the wild game animals had retreated into the forests to the north and west along with the native hunters.

The American Revolution, during which the Mohicans sided with the colonists, disrupted the years of relative peace. I thought it strange that my elementary and high school courses in American History had never mentioned any battles against the English in Westchester County, but all I have been able to find was one battle in White Plains and two "skirmishes" among colonial soldiers at taverns in Mount Vernon.

In the late 1800s, Irish, Italian, and other ethnic groups settled in New York City, which grew into a dense urban city. Had their competitive neighborhood and ethnic struggles gradually spilled out into the surrounding countryside? Had these struggles somehow soaked into the land and then been reborn in the form of our play fighting?

Half a century later, I returned to visit my old neighborhood and saw that although our apartment building remained, its surroundings had radically changed. Gone were the lawns, trees, and sandy playground; all replaced by a solid asphalt parking lot stretching from the street to the very walls of the building.

The vacant lot across the street was filled with tall apartment buildings jammed up right next to each other. Gone were any signs of children and their games; seemingly replaced by parked cars. *Gee,* I thought, *what do children do for fun now?* I imagined they were probably inside with air conditioning, TVs, computers, and maybe drugs. Were they fighting with each other? Were they watching wars on TV or playing war games on computer screens? Were they still listening to the prejudices of their parents? What remained or had changed since the times of Gramatan?

Chapter 4

ANGER AND ITS MANAGEMENT

Summers were wonderful. They were filled with days when the other children and I could play and then eat our sandwiches, milk, and fruit out on the large lawn behind our apartment building. One summer, though, our enjoyment was marred by one little boy who insisted on throwing grass into everyone else's milk.

One day, I had had enough, so I stood up and threw a wild punch in the direction of his face. To my amazement, it landed on his nose, which began to bleed profusely. That lucky punch had more repercussions than I could have imagined. Not only did he run home to his mother, but his mother got mad at my mother, and my mother yelled back at his mother, and the whole neighborhood talked about it. Then my mother told me his mother was a "whore." I had no idea what that was, but I knew it wasn't good. Bottom line: the little boy never threw grass in milk again. I concluded that the outcome was righteous justification for my lucky punch. Furthermore, my righteous anger was reinforced by the righteous anger of my own country, which was still at war in Europe. But can one-on-one bullying and righteous responses really be applied to whole societies of people?

One day in our apartment when I was probably about 7 or 8, I became very angry. Looking back, I can't remember why I was angry, but I do remember the explosion of that anger from my body. "Damn!" I screamed as I threw the windup handle across the room. And then, to my horror, I watched as it settled in slow motion upon a stack of seven phonograph records. And, yes, each of those beautiful classical records broke. Even worse, they weren't my records; a neighbor had lent them to me. Although I was eventually able to earn the money to pay for the damage, that lesson of unintended consequences caused by the explosion of my sudden anger was indelibly seared in my memory. It restrained many physical and verbal expressions of anger far into my middle and older decades. It probably led many people to describe me as "sweet." In hindsight, this lesson was both positive and negative. Positive because it prevented future dangers to me and others; negative because it bottled up feelings of righteous anger at great danger to my own self-respect.

One day in midcareer, a coworker and I stood and listened helplessly as the head of our department yelled at us disrespectfully and unjustly. I so wanted to clench my right fist and punch him in the nose. I managed to restrain myself because

I needed the job and certainly didn't want to end all chances of any job. I went home that evening, still feeling unjustly accused. The next morning, I found that a large patch of tiny red spots had broken out on the skin of my right shoulder and upper arm. A doctor diagnosed it as shingles and prescribed medicine, which was fortunately effective since I began using it within the first seventy-two hours. It seems most suspicious to me that the shingles virus had appeared exactly within the specific set of muscles, skin, and bone I had so consciously restrained from swinging a punch.

A few years later, I signed on to a class in the Korean martial art of Tae Kwon Do and learned more than expected about anger and self-defense. Beginning classes consisted of targeted stretching and "play fighting," with punches and kicks aimed into the air adjacent to opponents.

The day came when we had to hit each other directly, beginning with the unpadded instructor and then the padded students.

"I can't do it," I said.

"Why not?" asked the instructor.

"I might hurt you," I said.

The instructor, who appeared to have muscles of steel, laughed and said, "You're not going to hurt me!"

"But," I said, "I haven't hit anyone since the second grade."

After more coaching, I reluctantly hit him and finally hit the padded students. Midway through the next class, I suddenly realized that my muscles enjoyed the feeling of punching and kicking. *Oh my,* I thought. *Now I understand why people enjoy physical fighting, especially children like my three sons.* I then felt an unexpected empathy for children, especially for males at puberty who have hormonally strong muscles and feel a compelling need to physically fight.

Hmmm, I wondered. *What if wars could just be resolved with martial arts or other physical displays of strength? But then,* I asked myself, *what about other contests of worth such as engineering and the arts? And what about the health of people as a measure of the strength of a society?* Then, of course, I recognized that several thousands of years of warfare and street fights on our planet had been fed not only by strong and clever warriors but also by women continually giving birth to children and replacing those who had died, been injured, or simply aged.

One day the carpenter remodeling my bathroom had a verbal fight with an electrician. I had asked the carpenter to make a hole for a wall heater and had asked the licensed electrician to subsequently install it. The carpenter had agreed, but he had asked for the phone number of the electrician so he could confer about its size. That sounds simple, but the carpenter had gone a step further and described various details about the wiring and the heater I had bought. The electrician had then become angry, called him a "jerk," and said the carpenter had no legal right to do anything with electricity and that I had apparently ordered the wrong heater. They had further words; the electrician said he wouldn't be involved in any way with the job, and the carpenter hung up.

On hearing this account, I became angry at the electrician; after all, the carpenter had only been trying to be helpful. What did the electrician mean about the wrong heater being ordered? I had only ordered the one he had specified. Now I was without an electrician and apparently being blamed for ordering the wrong equipment. All that evening I felt ripples of anger starting in the pit of my stomach and spreading throughout my body. I hadn't been present, but their fight had affected and upsets me. Is anger contagious?

To understand and manage my own physical reactions, I considered the components of my own involvement and physical upset. There appeared to be two components of my physical feelings of being upset: Fear—someone thinks I am just a silly old woman who can't be relied on to order something; and anger—how dare he be rude to the carpenter, who was only trying to help?

Just acknowledging the components of my own fear and anger was somewhat calming. I waited until morning and then called the electrician to hear his side. He acknowledged that he might have overreacted but that he had become fed up with carpenters doing electrical work. I then explained that I had ordered the exact number of the wall heater he had specified. What had happened was that the high wattage label on the wall heater had been misleading by not including the smaller-print description allowing for the recommended lower-wattage setting. He accepted that explanation and acknowledged that none of this was my fault and that he would be happy to work on another job for me, just not this one because of possible complications initiated by someone else. The carpenter and electrician were still not speaking, and I had no way of knowing the accuracy of what each had reported about their confrontation. However, I felt physically calmer. Why? Because I knew I had investigated the situation as far as I could in my attempts to reconcile it; the rest had to be the responsibility of the other two people. So much conflict seemed to rise from misunderstandings that were complex and required patience and diligence to untangle even between two or three people.

Another time I wasn't so successful at anger management. I was on a beautiful sailing trip with friends amid the San Juan Islands off the coast of Washington State. One night we tied up at a dock and gathered around the small table for supper below deck. We were disturbed, however, by noxious oil fumes settling into our space. "Ugh," we all said. "Those fumes must be coming from the generator of that other boat." My friends said something like, "I hope they stop soon," but no one did anything. I suddenly became so angry at the idea of sitting and passively breathing in toxic fumes that I jumped up, climbed on deck, and stepped onto the dock.

I was on a righteous mission to end the source of the fumes. Unfortunately, I had forgotten to put my shoes on. My foot slipped on the wet dock, and I began to slide down between the dock and the boat. Rather than risk hitting my head on the boat or dock and possibly drowning, I threw myself forward. I managed to land flat on the dock with the brunt of the force on my head and right shoulder.

I was probably unconscious for a minute or so and then came to with an extremely sore shoulder. By that time, my friends had arrived, talked with the owners of the generator, and stopped the fumes. Mission accomplished! In my haste, though, I had retorn previously injured tendons in my rotator cuff. That second tearing of tendons cost me several more years of pain. What I learned from this painful lesson was that when reacting with righteous anger, I'd better put my shoes on first.

On September 11, 2001 (9/11), I watched the TV monitor as planes flew into the Twin Towers in New York City. I saw the flames, the smoke, the melting of the towers, and the people throwing themselves out the windows. Eerily, that horrible scene was like a scene I had previously watched, a scene in the movie *Star Wars*. In that scene, Luke Skywalker flies into the heart of the evil Empire, and it all blows up. *OMG*, I thought. *Someone thinks we are the evil Empire.*

I cried, but I never saw President Bush cry; he looked confused and then scared. And then he got angry. People around him got angry; they bombed the country of Afghanistan. Many people died, but at least women in Afghanistan no longer had to wear burkas, which covered and suffocated their whole bodies and souls. They could even go to schools and run for the legislature—that is, if they could escape the dictates of their own husbands and families. That war, our longest one, officially ended in 2021, the year in which I am completing this book. As I write, thousands of US soldiers, Afghan allies, and their families are being evacuated. It is the end of war, but it doesn't feel like peace.

As much as I hated war, I could understand the drive to bomb Afghanistan. But then the president and his administration went to war against the country of Iraq. Iraq? The pilots who flew those planes into the Twin Towers had come from Saudi Arabia, trained in Afghanistan, lived in Germany, and then learned to fly in Minnesota and Florida. I had watched the same TV as everyone else, but after just a few months of government officials talking about Iraq and 9/11, the anger of most of the country was redirected toward Iraq.

First, the president threatened the city of Baghdad with tremendous explosions, called "shock and awe." Those of us who couldn't understand why Baghdad was being threatened stood around a large fountain in Houston for many cold nights in February to silently protest. Our government bombed the city of Baghdad anyway. Victorious American tanks moved into Baghdad, and US soldiers helped topple statues of Saddam Hussein. US government officials and others celebrated.

The defeated Iraqi army went home with their guns but with no further paychecks. Then the marketplaces opened again, but now they could buy alcohol. *Oh, that's smart*, I thought. *Angry men with guns now have alcohol.* That "victorious" war has now morphed into new wars in the same region and more dead and more suffering. Sadness and tears are slow moving but at least allow time for thought processes. Anger is quick with no such time and less ability to predict consequences.

I'm still learning the art and science of expressing and responding to anger—whether of my own or other peoples' making and whether justified or not. These are my conclusions:

- It's best to examine the sources of your own physical feelings of anger.
- Fear is an important precursor of anger.

- Words and punches can both be weapons, and each has its place.
- Bombs and missiles are rarely "pinpoint" in their targeting.
- Be sure to put your shoes on before responding to threats.

Chapter 5

PRAYER AND YEARNING

(Please note: The lesson described in this chapter is based on my own experiences and perceptions. It is not intended to challenge the beliefs of others who have had different experiences and perceptions.)

As a well-trained young Catholic, I said my prayers every night with several memorized standards, such as the Lord's Prayer and Hail Mary. These were followed by what I would now call "wish prayers," such as "Please help me ..." or "Please let me have ..."

The nuns taught me that these wish prayers would be especially affective if directed to Mary, since she was the "mother of God," and "Jesus was so perfect that he wouldn't want to grant anything without his mother's approval." This seemed a little odd to me and further confused my understanding of Jesus; Mary; the Holy Ghost; God, the omnipotent;

and so forth. Accordingly, I only occasionally said such prayers and reserved them for what I considered to be important and non-material items, such as, "Please make my father well again. Please let my mother be happy. Please help me to stop fighting with my brother."

Yet I had deep yearnings within myself I had never voiced or expressed in prayer since they didn't seem even remotely possible. Those yearnings were to live in the woods, mountains, and streams I had been reading about in books and experiencing in small doses in the lawns and trees of our suburban town.

I also longed for a father. Although I had a biological father, I hadn't seen him for over three years, because he was in a hospital with TB, and I wasn't allowed to visit him. In those times, the 1940s, there were no medicines that were effective against the highly contagious tuberculosis bacterium, and children weren't allowed to visit hospitals because of their own communicable childhood diseases. Letters and phone calls were allowed, but letters lacked voice and touch and had a time delay, while phone calls to a shared phone in a hallway were technically difficult and expensive.

Then one day, to my incredible surprise, my deep yearnings to be in more natural settings and have a physically close father figure became a reality. A friend of my grandmother, whom I had never even met, invited my mother, brother, and me to housesit for him in the mountains of western Pennsylvania for August. Since we didn't own a car, his invitation even included driving us there during his return trip from business in New York City.

Suddenly I was living the life about which I had been reading and dreaming. I was waking up to days surrounded by
fields and woods, swimming and fishing in a creek, watching cows, falling in love with frogs as I walked along a creek,
swimming with other children in that same creek, meeting
new people, and hearing new stories with new ideas and
new accents.

And how was it that I received this gift through no prayers
or other efforts of my own? It was because my grandmother
had once befriended someone when he most needed it. This
kind and cheerful man, whom I called "Uncle," loved fine
china, crystal, linens, and antiques. He owned a small factory,
where he hired women to embroider tablecloths, which provided needed employment in that rural area. He lived with
another man, whom I also grew to love and call "Uncle." I
wasn't aware that these interests or living arrangements were
unusual; I was simply appreciating everyone and everything
in this new setting. Years later I understood more about the
whole picture, and I marveled at how he and his partner had
managed to thrive and share their love within the straitlaced
and less tolerant culture of the 1950s.

Another amazing gift fulfilled my childhood yearnings
for cowboys, horses, and fields of waving grasses. Most of
these fantasies had come from books and then from the
stage play *Oklahoma*, which had opened with a glorious
scene of bright yellow sunshine and waving wheat. (This
can be genuinely appreciated only if one has just come in
out of a cold, gray driving New York sleet.) I had been exploring possibilities of college both in the northeast and

other states, such as the somewhat fantastical idea of the University of Oklahoma.

I wanted to get away from the northeast partly, not only because its colleges were expensive but also because I was anxious to explore other parts of the world. I was also irritated because I had learned from my schoolmates that most of those colleges had quotas limiting the number of Jewish students. In addition, I was passionate about history, but most of the northeastern colleges appeared to have only American and European history courses. In contrast, the University of Oklahoma was inexpensive, had no quotas and offered history courses that included Latin America and Asia. This was the place to which I was drawn, but it was so far away that I didn't even bother to wish or pray for it.

Then another amazing event occurred, for which I could take no credit. My mother was sitting in the showroom of the wholesale gift business she had inherited from my grandmother. She had just wound up a toy cat and was idly watching it roll around on the floor when a man walked in, attracted by the toy cat. He explained that he was from Oklahoma and that his son went to the University of Oklahoma, which he said was an up-and-coming university. The more they talked, the more my mother became comfortable with the possibility of the three of us moving to Oklahoma, where the cost of living would be less and where I could attend the university without having to pay out-of-state tuition.

In the spring of my senior year in high school, I applied and was accepted to the University of Oklahoma. We then investigated and wrote letters of inquiry to towns that were small but not too small. We decided on the city of Muskogee, the only one to respond with an informational and welcoming letter.

That summer I could hardly contain my excitement as we weeded out and packed up our remaining belongings. Suddenly we were flying and then landing in the hottest and driest place I had ever experienced. Hot, it was, but we were soon meeting new people, who welcomed us to Muskogee and showed us the local swimming pool. That was the first time in my life that I was able to swim and not be cold the minute I got out of the pool. Then we had our first experience of a drive-in movie theatre. I've forgotten the movie but not what I saw when I left the car to go to the concession stand— it was so unexpected that I gasped; millions of stars appeared to be just over my head.

Further surprises in Oklahoma began with hearing people say, "Y'all come back now!" I heard them speaking with an accent but also learned I had an accent. In addition to accent differences, I unexpectedly learned that the normal way my friends and I had talked in New York, with clever putdowns of each other, wasn't the way people in Oklahoma talked. Their faces expressed true shock when I made my perfectly normal sarcastic comments.

Within a few weeks, I began university life, in which courses in geology and Oklahoma history opened my eyes to unexpected worlds. Geology gave me the ability to see not just the land around me but its origins and history—rivers carving out caves and eroding mountains into the sea, wind and sand creating massive shapes, molten rock building land, and minerals fossilizing life. I learned that the history of humans in Oklahoma had arisen not just from Indians of the plains but from settled peoples in the mountains of Georgia, the Carolinas, Tennessee, and Florida. New to me was their Trail of Tears, which hadn't been mentioned in the American history books of my high school.

These and many additional gifts have come to me without conscious wishing or praying—only deep yearning followed by reasonable effort. I have concluded that one need not dismiss any dreams as "impossible" and that conscious work toward those goals may lead in unexpected directions. Most important is to recognize and be grateful for the arrival of unexpected gifts.

Part Two

IN BETWEEN

Chapter 6

SUMMER LOVE

My first romance began during my seventeenth summer when I became a counselor at a YMCA camp in Connecticut. I had never been to an "away camp," and now I was not only going to one but also being paid for it. I had consciously prepared for this job by swimming farther than I had ever thought possible and learning how to free myself from the imagined holds of drowning people, which led to my certification as a lifeguard. I had obtained references to my character from teachers and neighbors, written letters, and filled out lots of applications. Now I could hardly contain my excitement as I boarded a bus to travel *by myself* to the mountains of Connecticut.

On the evening of my arrival, the other new counselors and I met for supper. In my usually private (some would call it shy) way, I simply went in and sat down by myself at one of the long tables. Someone named Joanie sat next to me; we found out we had a lot to talk about, and we became friends for the rest of our time at the camp. After dessert, a man, one of the adult counselors, approached me and said I had amazing blue eyes. *Huh*, I thought. *Why does everyone always remark about my blue eyes? I haven't done anything to earn them; they were just part of me when I arrived. Why doesn't anyone ever compliment me for something I have accomplished?* Nevertheless, I mumbled something else aloud and enjoyed an interesting conversation, the first among many, with this man.

My days were filled with responsibilities for the eight children in my cabin, shared meals, ceremonies, social hours with other counselors, and nightly campfires with singing and storytelling. We and my young campers told jokes, cleaned our cabin on Saturdays, and somehow managed to chase out the dust bunnies. We all slept in a cabin of bunk beds with wooden panels that opened to let in the air. How wonderful it was to lie at night, breathing in the clean, open air and listening to the night sounds.

In the mornings, we went to breakfast, had a daily ceremony, and went to various activities—me to teach swimming and be a lifeguard. Lifeguarding required continuously counting heads to be sure no one was missing. Being on the dock had the bonus of being next to the canoeing classes, and of course I jumped at the chance for free lessons.

One of the oddest things happened during the counselors' social hour. I followed the other counselors, who all gathered in a room away from the children to talk and smoke. At that time, most people smoked, but I didn't. I couldn't stand the coughing in my throat and burning in my eyes. I hated

being in that smoke-filled room when there was such beautiful fresh air outside, but I also very much wanted to be part
of the group. Sadly, I stayed with the group and put up with
burning eyes and throat.

Meanwhile, the man I had met at supper and I found more
things to talk about. He had graduated from college, had
been an army photographer during the Korean War, and was
now studying to be a minister. He had also traveled around
the United States, learning the dances of different Native
American tribes, and he even performed some of the dances
at the next campfire. He was twenty-six years old. *Gulp, that's
nine or ten years older than I!* I thought, but that didn't prevent
the warm feelings I had whenever we were together, nor the
warm, tingly sensations in my groin. My thoughts grew and
grew into dreams of hugging and kissing and then . . . the
dreams became real. In my first romance, we hugged and
kissed along paths, under trees, and in a boathouse.

As if all these new relationships and activities weren't ex-
citing enough, a rare hurricane traveled up the East Coast and
came ashore in Connecticut. Electricity, phones, and bridges
were knocked out, and the camp was isolated for three days
(no cell phones then). We had plenty of food and no other
problems, so the camp directors directed us to use rocks to
spell out "OK" for the search planes. We celebrated the first
day of the return of postal service with a meal, at which admission required that everyone present a letter to his or her
parents.

My love life continued but with nagging doubts about
how this could be possible with someone so much older. Then

one day my doubts were unexpectedly resolved. We were sitting on a rock by the lake when he suddenly said, "I need to tell you something … I am engaged to be married next year."

His words hit me like a shockwave. I was completely speechless and stunned. I felt as if I had been punched in my heart. I pictured hurling myself into the lake, yet I didn't. I stammered something. He said he was sorry. We walked away. I later learned from my friend, Joannie, that the other male counselors were talking about what a rotten thing he had done to me. *Guys have been talking about me?* (Yup, girls talk, and guys talk.)

The camp ended. I lived with the hurt and anger, but I lived. My heart didn't actually break; it healed but with a scar. I went on and had other wonderful and not-so-wonderful experiences with other loves. Some of them ended, and other scars formed in my heart. Sadly, I sometimes created scars in other hearts. Sometimes another person and I had feelings for each other before we really knew much about each other or really knew much about ourselves. Sometimes people I was attracted to already had another person they loved, and sometimes I had another person I loved. I wondered why we couldn't love more than one person of the opposite sex at the same time. Sometimes there really was lying and selfishness, but mostly it was just people learning and growing.

Twice the men I loved died. After the first such death, I rapidly fell in love with another man, who was a mutual friend. Part of me felt that this wasn't being loyal to my lover who had died, but I also felt that life was short and that nothing would bring him back to life. One night while getting ready for bed,

I had the strangest feeling. I physically felt that my lover who had died was embracing me and then spinning away while laughing.

Ironically, my next lover, who became my second husband, lived just five years more, which was the exact amount of time I had had with my previous lover. When he also died, I felt like I had been stabbed in my heart. Then one night while reading in our living room, I suddenly had a brief sensation that he, too, was sitting and reading in the other chair. In one memorable dream, he appeared as a Roman gladiator, taking my arm and explaining, "They get the best athletes by scaring us to death". Ultimately, what did all these loves and endings mean? With each death or ending of loves or deep friendships, I have felt both deep hurt and anger, but my rock-solid conviction has been to go on living and loving while the scars in my heart slowly heal and I experience new and wonderful relationships.

Chapter 7

THE LIFEGUARD ON DUTY

No, this isn't about the handsome young male lifeguard I fell in love with and then married and lived with happily ever—or not. I never actually married such a person. This is about me, the one who always loved swimming and learned to be truly at home in the water. Thanks to the YMCA, I began swimming lessons in elementary school and continued through high school, when I began lifeguard training. To qualify, I had to swim ten lengths of the pool without stopping—something I had never done before; but steady breathing and movement plus sheer determination paid off, and I did it.

Unexpectedly, my first lesson in lifeguard training wasn't about jumping in to save someone; it was about how to protect myself. I learned that a rescuer reaching for a victim could put himself or herself in danger. A panicky drowning person will grab on to anyone who approaches him or her and in the process, pull the rescuer under so there are now two drowning victims. Thus, the first lesson was to put some object between myself and the drowning person. A buoyant ring, a float, a paddle, a branch; even a towel would extend my reach while keeping me out of the reach of the victim.

Subsequent lessons addressed what to do if the only option was to dive in after someone. Those lessons were a fascinating combination of physics embedded in martial arts. The first trick was to approach the person from behind before grabbing him or her across the chest, securing the person on one hip, and using a side stroke to swim to safety with his or her flailing arms aimed in the opposite direction. If the only option was a frontal approach, one was taught to first dive under the water where the victim wouldn't want to go and then come up behind him or her. These life-saving movements took many hours and days of practice with a continued emphasis on self-protection.

Another basic principle wasn't quite so dramatic but equally critical. That was the discipline of keeping a constant watch on swimmers when on lifeguard duty. Watching thirty, forty, or one hundred or more active children and teenagers was both visually and mentally challenging. We were taught to constantly count people in the water to avoid suddenly missing someone. Meanwhile, there were some young ones, mostly boys, who just had to run on wet tile or cement and then jump off the side of the diving board, bringing them perilously close to the sides of the pool. Another challenge, again involving boys, was their game of "ducking" a girl's head under the water until she almost drowned or the lifeguard blew the whistle. This dangerous situation wasn't improved when the young girl came up, red faced and gasping but also giggling.

When I wasn't having to blow my whistle at these potential dangers, I was having to fight the tendency for my attention to wander off into daydreams. For months each summer, I practiced constantly refocusing on moving bodies, ready to respond if my greatest fear actually came to pass—someone truly in danger of drowning. And then on the last day of one summer swim season, it happened.

I noticed two young girls hanging onto the side of the pool while gradually moving into the deep end. I told them they would be allowed to go into the deep end only if they could show me that they could swim across the pool. This they did, but I could see that one of them was an especially weak swimmer. They had passed the test, though, so both were now in deep water, where I continued to keep a close eye on them. Then the weaker one got into trouble and panicked.

My entire body and mind responded in a flash as I dove into the water, put my arm around her from behind, placed her on my hip, swam to the edge, and pulled her out. I then made sure she and her friend were all right. I stood up, and then my knees began to shake. Whew! All that training and attention had paid off, and a tragedy had been averted. This occurrence dramatically demonstrated to me the presence and value of muscle memory throughout the body when there is no time for the mind to debate about actions.

Lifeguard training unexpectedly averted another tragedy many decades later. I was with a tour group on a small boat in Italy when it stopped at a cove filled with beautiful, cool, blue-green water. Having been assured by the captain that this was a fine place to swim, about half a dozen of us jumped into the water. The cold initially shocked me, but I warmed up as I began moving my arms and legs while enjoying the feeling of being immersed in such beauty.

Suddenly, a woman about six to eight feet away began screaming, "Help, the current is pulling me away; bring the boat back." I immediately began assessing the situation and debating what to do. The boat captain appeared to be oblivious to what was happening as the boat was slowly drifting away. Although I had once saved a child from drowning, this was a large woman, and I was now over eighty years old. *Do not rush in*, I reflexively said to myself. *But what should I do*?

Was there anything to throw or extend to her? No. I saw, though, that she wasn't actually sinking. I had previously learned, when I had been caught in currents, that by not letting my legs sink, I could remain on the surface of the water where the current had less effect. Although she appeared to be too weak to swim against the current, she was at least floating vertically. I sought, therefore, to convince her that she could get on top of the current. I called her name in my most commanding voice, saying, "Lean back. Lean back!"

Finally, amid persistent cries of "I can't" and "I'm too weak," she leaned back, which put her on the surface.

Then I quickly added, "Kick your legs!" Amid continued protestations of weakness, she slowly progressed toward the boat, while I paralleled her progress from a safe distance. Then I said, "Turn around. You're at the boat."

She managed to pull herself up the ladder and then collapsed into the boat, meanwhile saying, "Thank you, thank you; you saved my life." This time my knees didn't shake, but I did heave a huge sigh of relief.

Although these lifeguarding lessons about focused attention and avoiding the clutches of a drowning person have twice paid off, I have often forgotten them when confronted by other types of drowning victims—those drowning in emotional problems. Family arguments, workplace misunderstandings, school bullying, alcoholism, drug addictions, physical and mental diseases, or just bad luck create so many victims and so many would-be rescuers.

Too often I have rushed in to help but then been sucked into situations I didn't fully understand, only to become the second drowning victim. After several lengthy "drowning" situations, in which I became both emotionally and physically sick, I woke up to the messages of others, who had learned from these situations. Books such as *The Dance of Anger*[3] and support groups such as Al Anon[4] gave me insights into long-term patterns of dysfunctional behavior and co-dependency that had existed in my own family and other relationships. I now try to carefully assess cries for help and maintain my own safety before rushing in to help. It may take me another lifetime to truly learn this type of safer and probably more effective help, but I'm working on it.

Part Three

THE WONDERS AND PITFALLS OF ADULTHOOD

Chapter 8

LOVE, SEX, BABIES, AND WAR

During my college years, I craved sex. The expression for craving sex back then was "horny"; I don't know where that expression came from or what the current expression is. At that time, there was no sex allowed outside of marriage—zero, zip, nada—at least not for women. College dormitories were separated by gender, and the women's dorms had a house mother, who locked the door at ten p.m. on weekdays and eleven p.m. on weekends. Arriving after hours was a serious offense, and too many such arrivals might result in dismissal from school. Meanwhile, there were rumors of wild goings-on in the men's dorms—especially those among the athletes, including drinking, sex, and prostitution.

My body cried out so desperately for something to enter my vagina and plunge deep within my being that sometimes in the middle of class I broke out into a cold sweat. Obviously, this was extremely distracting. Yet I never even considered the possibility of sex without marriage due to the fear of pregnancy and strong social shame. Of course, disease would have also been a risk but was less talked about in those days. Disease was limited to syphilis and gonorrhea, since HIV and AIDS hadn't yet arrived. I had never even heard the word *masturbation* until I read it in a book and found its definition to be "self-abuse," so it never crossed my mind as an option.

I had various short-term boyfriends, and we enjoyed hugs, kisses, and what was then known as "necking" but no actual sex. During the last semester of college, I moved into the apartment of a friend within a large older home divided into about six different apartments. These apartments were owned by a farmer in western Oklahoma and managed by one of his three sons to help pay for the college education of himself and his two brothers. *Hmmm*, I thought. *This is a smart family.*

One day the apartment manager came to retile our bathroom. I had never seen anything retiled and was fascinated with the process, so I insisted on helping. "This is very precise work," he insisted, "so you probably don't have the necessary skill for it." Nevertheless, I persisted and was hesitatingly allowed to lay a few tiles, which I managed successfully. This was to be the first of many such Tom Sawyer-like moments, in which I begged to participate in new skills and work involving painting, carpentry, Sheetrock floating, and even car repair.

It was all fascinating to me after growing up in a rented apartment, in which our family wasn't responsible for repairing or remodeling anything. I had never even known that walls were composed of Sheetrock and pieces of lumber. These basic skills sessions were a wonderful way for two somewhat shy people to become acquainted. We had a whirlwind romance that included sex before marriage since we were convinced that sex was beautiful and that we could be responsible adults using birth control.

Our first year of marriage included his last year of an engineering major and my first year of teaching. Teaching was stressful for me, but that's another story. We became acquainted with each other's families and had sex—lots of wonderful sex! As soon as I was finally having regular sex, thoughts of having a baby rose in my mind. Although I had never been interested in dolls, I had always been fascinated by babies. The more sex we had, the more I craved becoming pregnant; and in our second year of marriage, we stopped using birth control, and I became pregnant.

Pregnancy was a fascinating experience, in which I read everything I could to inform myself. The birth of our first child took place in New Orleans in May 1962. I had a relatively short (five hours) natural childbirth experience, which was a revolutionary act at that time. However, nothing I had read or heard prepared me for those first months with a new baby.

In my case, my coccyx (tailbone) had fractured during the delivery, likely because it had been curved forward rather than backward. It didn't hurt during the birth itself when I heard only a loud crack, but it hurt for two years afterward. My vision of peacefully rocking while nursing was unexpectedly scrapped because sitting hurt too much. I have memories of leaning against walls while nursing in the middle of the night. Nothing could be done about my tailbone according to my doctor. Pain medicines, which weren't so prevalent at that time, never occurred to me or the doctor, and I'm glad they didn't since I was nursing.

My second shock related to nursing was that its highly recommended health benefits for my baby were replaced with sessions of screaming with colic. The one time he didn't have colic was the time my husband gave him a bottle of formula. The pediatrician had no idea why this was occurring or what to do about it because it was rare for mothers to nurse at that time. Books on baby care also had no advice. I was also relying on the authoritative teaching in a biology course that the mother's milk had already been rendered ideal for the baby.

The first helpful knowledge that came to me occurred over two years later when I told my mother-in-law about my fears of repeat colic with our second baby. "Well, Nancy," she said, "we older mothers don't like to interfere with the newer generation of parents who have access to modern scientific advice, but in our days of nursing, we knew there were certain foods to avoid because they were apt to cause colic. You know, coffee, chocolate, garlic, brussels sprouts, and broccoli."

Following my mother-in-law's advice while nursing our next child, I avoided coffee and chocolate and watched for any reactions after eating the other foods. Our second and third babies had no problems with colic. My subsequent scientific education taught me that this was only "anecdotal" evidence, so it couldn't be extrapolated into guidance for all new mothers. Fortunately, however, breastfeeding has become more commonly practiced so there has been more research. Gas-forming vegetables for adults are no longer suspect while caffeine, alcohol, soy, and cow milk are associated with risks of digestive and other reactions for some babies. Reliable sources of support and information for new mothers can now be found through the La Leche League.[5]

Our second child was born in Milwaukee, Wisconsin, on a June day in 1965 after I had completed every item on my to-do list. He was a large baby at over eight pounds, but I was strong and used my breath and muscles to deliver him naturally. This time my tailbone didn't break thanks to an obstetrician who managed to guide the baby's head around it. Childbirth is truly an Olympic athletic experience requiring strength in addition to knowledge, breathing skills, and coordination. I recovered nicely and this time enjoyed a calm period of nursing, while his older brother played with neighborhood children.

The following autumn, our relatively calm life was unexpectedly altered when the large double-paned living room window cracked. Although we hadn't broken it, the landlord assumed we had and evicted us. Suddenly, we were having to search for a new place to live in a city where most rental places didn't allow children. Discrimination against families with children became illegal three years later with the passage of the federal Fair Housing Act, which also prohibited discrimination based on race, color, religion, sex, disability, or national origin.[6] Just before winter arrived, we managed to find another place less insulated but adequate.

This was during the time of the war in Vietnam. Thanks to

my brother, who was attending the University of Wisconsin and accessing a wider variety of news sources than I, I learned news beyond that of the local newspaper, which seemed to be limited to Pentagon press releases. These additional sources showed photographs of villages destroyed by US firepower along with horrible deaths and injuries.

I became more and more upset by what my own government was doing in the name of "fighting communism." One day someone handed me a leaflet, inviting me to join a group that was opposed to the war. I immediately signed on and went to a meeting that included about six other people. We discussed what to do and decided to first try to get the facts and then to sponsor a debate between two college professors with pro and con views about the war. My task was to clip out all articles about the war from the *Milwaukee Journal*. We then compared them to other sources, such as a small monthly newsletter by I. F. Stone, who pointed out inconsistencies within reports from the pentagon and White House.

Each day was filled with caring for a baby and a three-year-old, cleaning, cooking, and washing dishes by hand; and I had just become pregnant again. Nevertheless, I felt that I had to do something about this war. My husband agreed to care for the children in the evenings so I could join another woman to publicize our planned debate about the war. She and I spent the next two months of a typically cold Milwaukee winter knocking on doors to ask opinions and invite people to the debate.

Typical responses included "Our government has experts to make these decisions" and "That's so sweet of you ladies to come out in the cold, but this is something the men need to figure out." Similar statements were echoed on radio call-in shows and seem shockingly naïve now. They need to be seen, though, against the backdrop of the early 1960s before anti-war protests had begun and before the rebirth of the women's movement. Although the cold war with the Soviet Union had been simmering along for about two decades, this was the first dropping of bombs and drafting of men (just men) to fight. Most people expressed true shock that any patriotic American would even question the decisions of government officials and their "experts." What a contrast to today, when it seems so normal to question anything and everything about the government.

After two months of canvassing in the cold, the synagogue where the debate was to be held canceled the event. We scrambled to find another place, and the two professors engaged in a scholarly and reasonable debate, but with no time for publicity, not one of the hundreds of invitees attended. We were frustrated and discouraged, but we continued with protests and silent vigils—against a backdrop of cold winds blowing off Lake Michigan. Did I mention it was cold?

In the meantime, my constant going out at night for anti-war work and being distracted by the radio news during the day were stressful for me, my husband, and our two small children. My mind was traveling along parallel tracks: wartime horror and fascination with our two growing children and a third pregnancy. There was something about pregnancy, childbirth, babies, and toddlers that fascinated me regardless of my broken leg veins, boredom with house cleaning, and my longing to be in a world of other adults in fascinating careers.

During the following June of 1967, our third child was born in another natural childbirth. Although our second child was only two years old and still in diapers, which added to the challenge of a new baby, I felt I had finally acquired the skills necessary for nursing and infant care. Two months later, we moved to Dallas, where my husband began a new job. We were still young and strong, and we felt like we could handle everything. Six months later, though we were challenged by the chicken pox in all three children, and this was followed by the flu for all of us. (The chapter "A Time to Be Born, or Not" describes this especially serious challenge for me.)

Still, the war in Vietnam continued and continued to mess with my head. A year and a half later, we moved to Houston, where I continued going to anti-war protests. Ironically, I began to note that my marches for peace were too often followed by my own small sons fighting at home. *What is going on?* I wondered. I read books on child raising and asked more experienced parents.

"Don't worry about it," they said. "It's just like puppies fighting." But I did worry; we had a few trips to the emergency room, and I had a hard time dealing with the constant noise and arguing. Long before becoming a parent, I had sworn that I would never spank my children as I had been spanked as a child. Nowhere, though, had I learned any alternatives for getting the attention of small children to maintain some order and safety. I was reduced to instinctive yelling, which wasn't much of an improvement. One day I yelled so much that I gave myself a headache.

Years later I learned about alternative methods of discipline from our grown sons and their wives. The first alternative was the concept of the time-out with the length of time based on the age of the child. What a good idea! The times I saw it being used for my grandchildren seemed to be effective and at least were quiet. I then remembered that my mother had used a version of this method on me, but it had been for hours at a time locked in my bedroom. I'm not sure how much good it did because I simply had spent the time thinking about how unfair it was and how I was being so mistreated.

The second alternative was a set of concepts I learned in a class in the martial art of Tae Kwon Do. The physical skills of fighting were taught along with respect for an opponent. Although fighting was the object of the class, it didn't rule the class. Combatants bowed to each other before and after each match. Hits to the head and below the belt were off limits. Absent were the arguments, injuries, and chaos of our home-grown fighting.

Unexpectedly, I also learned the appeal of physical fighting. When we first began to practice hitting each other, we were well padded, but our instructors were not. "Hit me," said the instructor.

"I can't," I said.

"Why not?" he said.

"I haven't hit anyone since the second grade, and I might hurt you."

He laughed and said, "You're not going to hurt me!" I hesitatingly accepted the reality that my delicate hands would be unlikely to do much against his steel-like chest.

I then overcame my decades of feminine training and hit

him and then hit the other instructor and then hit various padded students. In a flash, I realized that hitting and kicking were fun and that it felt good to be using my newly developed strength and coordination in the art of fighting. *Oh my God*, I thought. *Perhaps this is one reason why so many children fight.*

Developing muscles need something to test their strength against, and puberty, especially for boys with increasing levels of testosterone, must enhance that need in irresistible ways. How much better to recognize and respect this drive to fight while channeling it into the various forms of martial arts and other sports.

War, however, has evolved far beyond the physical arts of fighting. War now seems to be less about physical strength and more about engineering, hardware and explosives. Deaths occur among noncombatants along with starvation and the pollution of whole populations of people, animals, and plants. War is now out of control with few, if any, redeeming qualities.

As I write this section, I witness televised scenes of the end of twenty years of war in Afghanistan. Panic and chaos and injuries and deaths surround an airport as thousands try to flee. When the airport escape route closes, desperate refugees flee to the borders of other countries, near and far. Some remain trapped. Girls can no longer go to schools and women lose jobs.

Peace should not look like this, but I cannot fault the leaders and advisors who have finally said, "Enough is enough". I am forced to acknowledge the complexity of human conflicts multiplied by different cultures and subcultures. Recognizing the basic human rights of people of all ethnicities and genders should be obvious, but apparently it is not. Even with the best of intentions and technology, effectively supporting the rights of people in other societies can be especially problematic.

Chapter 9

A TIME TO BE
BORN, OR NOT

Pregnancies for all three of our children were planned; they were relatively healthy, and the births were anxiously and joyfully awaited. I managed the usual morning sicknesses, kept physically active, and ate as well as I knew how. There were three years between our first and second child, which was a smart plan because at three years, our older child was out of diapers and had a well-developed vocabulary and neighborhood playmates. The subsequent two years between our second and third child weren't a smart plan. At two years, our older child was still in diapers, had a limited vocabulary, and was more attached to me.

With each pregnancy, the veins in my legs suffered from the added weight on my slim five-foot-three frame. By the end of my third pregnancy, broken veins had spread all the way down both legs. They were not only ugly but also painful. I couldn't stand up when I woke in the morning unless I first pulled on heavy elastic stockings that were tight, hot, and generally uncomfortable. Six months after the birth of our third child, I still had to wear those heavy-duty elastic stockings, even though I had lost a lot of weight. I was nursing our third baby, but unlike when I had nursed the first two babies, my milk was no longer flowing in abundance. I was also physically and mentally exhausted.

In addition to my compromised health, our second child was competing with his older brother for toys and couldn't understand why I couldn't devote more of my time to him rather than to his baby brother. We had just moved from Milwaukee to Dallas for my husband's new job, which was positive in many ways but also challenging. Then all three children caught the chicken pox. A vaccine against it had become available that year, and they had each been vaccinated, but each broke out with symptoms the very next day. Had they gotten the chicken pox from the vaccine? I'll never know because this was also at the same time of a city-wide epidemic.

We unwisely decided to continue our Christmas plans to visit our families in Oklahoma when the itchy and miserable symptoms appeared, and their two cousins then caught the chicken pox. We had barely made it back home when all of us came down with the flu, for which there was no vaccine or medicine at that time. Somehow my husband managed to keep going to work, where he probably spread it further. I struggled out of bed each morning and continued cooking, cleaning, nursing the baby, and feeding myself and the rest of the family. I couldn't seem to get warm and huddled on the floor by our small gas heater, while the two older children cried, whined, and fought with each other.

A couple of months later, all of us had somehow recovered, but both my husband and I remained exhausted for several more months. I had weaned the baby and begun taking birth control pills; however, I had also begun working in a Montessori preschool. Each day required seeing the oldest child off to first grade, taking the baby to a babysitter, and bringing the middle child to the same preschool where I worked. This made for complicated and full days, which I had chosen because of my fascination with the Montessori philosophy of childhood learning and desperation to get out of the house and be with other adults. While rushing around to leave on three of those days, I forgot to take my birth control pills. Had I overloaded myself with such a schedule? Yes. Was it my responsibility and error in forgetting those pills? Yes. Three weeks later, my menstrual period didn't arrive.

Oh my God! I can't be pregnant now!

Abortion wasn't legal in any of the United States at that time, and medical exceptions were rare even for women with serious health threats including cancer. However, some women still got abortions, and I had heard many stories of horrible consequences in illegal settings or on trips to Mexico. The country of Sweden had recently legalized abortion, but we didn't have the kind of money that would have allowed for such a trip with medical care and a day or days in a hotel.

I knew my body and mind couldn't withstand one more pregnancy and that I was barely managing to care for the three closely spaced children we already had. For two weeks, I waited in a state of constant terror until my period finally, blessedly came. Whew! I had narrowly avoided a real tragedy that would have had unhealthy and dangerous consequences for me and my entire family. I never again forgot to take those pills and finally had a tubal ligation.

Never have I forgotten those two weeks of terror. That memory drove me onto the streets many times with a sign supporting a woman's right to choose, and I continue to donate money to this cause. How could someone else dare to make such a momentous decision for my own body and mind?

Why was it that governments and most religions could support armies of men (and now women) who killed in support of their homelands and then welcome them back as heroes? Even in civilian life, someone who kills an attacker has the right to claim self-defense. Yet when a woman in defense of her own body needs to end the life of an unborn child, she isn't granted this same right.

The right to an abortion was finally gained in 1972, but this right has been increasingly curtailed, and efforts to obtain an abortion are often delayed, which is especially cruel as each hour and day brings a fetus closer to the point of feeling. The birth of a child can be a beautiful thing, but there is a time to be born (or not), and the person giving consent needs to be the one carrying and birthing the new baby.

Chapter 10

HISTORY AND HER STORY

I majored in history during college because I loved hearing stories about life before I had been born. How had we all arrived at this time and place with such interesting cultures? Courses in the histories of Oklahoma, Asia, Latin America, and Russia greatly broadened my horizons. Additional courses in the Protestant Reformation, Social History of the US, and the History of Science provided insights beyond typical military-political events. Although I was fascinated with the stories of the major players in history, no matter what type of history I studied, those stories were mostly "his story"—kings, presidents, generals, composers, scientists, and inventors— with only rare stories of queens, nurses, or women as martyrs.

In those days, male students with degrees in history could begin careers in teaching, governmental services, or news reporting and analysis. There were no women reporters or

analysts on TV or radio. None. Such jobs weren't even imaginable for a woman, especially one who was planning on marriage and children. My career opportunities were limited to
being a secretary, nurse, or teacher. Secretaries weren't like
today's office managers; they were chiefly limited to taking
dictation and typing. Nursing initially attracted me, but nurses
were almost always women. When I learned that they had to
stand whenever an almost-always male doctor entered the
room, I had no desire to put myself in such a position. I knew
that at some point my temper would cause me to "disrespectfully" lash out and lose a job. Accordingly, I began a career as
a high school history teacher, chiefly because it seemed the
least objectionable of my three choices.

As a new teacher in a small-town school, I wasn't broken
in easily; I was assigned four different subjects: world history,
Oklahoma history, English, and geography plus hall duty in
place of a lunch break. I quickly became overwhelmed with
such varied class preparation, grading of tests, and unexpected issues involving order in the classroom.

First, I discovered that several high school students
couldn't read and that others had hearing or vision problems, about which I hadn't been warned. On further inquiry, I
learned that a larger school district five miles away routinely
referred their students with learning difficulties to our small
school district. Our district was happy to accept them because
it increased the size of their student population, which yielded
an increase in state aid. They couldn't, however, afford to provide any specialized services for these students.

Discipline was the elephant in the room that had never

been examined or even mentioned during my courses in education. My introduction to discipline in the school was learning that I was to send any unruly students to the principal,
who would beat them with a split baseball bat! I refused to
cooperate with this brutal system, and some students took
this as a sign that they could get away with anything in my
classroom, which rapidly descended into chaos. I had major
confrontations with the principal and superintendent concerning chaos in my class, my refusal to do hall duty during
my lunch hour, and concern about the lack of support for students with learning difficulties. At the end of the first semester, I resigned in a major state of frustration and exhaustion.
This was the first time in my life I had ever quit anything.

After a stint in graduate school—thinking college teaching might be the answer—three pregnancies, and anger
about the war in Vietnam, I read *The Feminine Mystique*.[7] This
book was the first to clearly express and reinforce my own
barely conscious irritations and chafing under the "natural"
assignment of gender roles; it was *her* story! It told the stories
of women not deemed important enough to have been acknowledged in the history books of my time: Harriet Tubman,
Susan B. Anthony, and more. I read about the male bias of
textbooks that had routinely made fun of women suffrag-
ettes. I suddenly felt tears running down my face as I realized
I had been one of the many students laughing at those "silly
women."

I wasn't alone in my growing rebellion. First, a close
woman friend and then more and more women began to
question their roles. By the early 1970s, I had joined both the

newly formed National Organization for Women and an infor-
mal consciousness-raising group. Suddenly, other women and
I were uncovering layers of resentment about our assumed
roles of weakness, subservience, and victimhood.

We unearthed buried stories of heroic women who had
gone before us. We confronted our fears of rape and un-
planned pregnancies. We learned about women who had
died from sexual attacks but also about ones who had fought
back and survived. We learned about the hushed-up stories
of women who had had illegal abortions and then either died
or survived with or without regrets.

I acknowledged that I had accepted a limited and weak
role for myself and had feared appearing to look strong. In
school I had accepted the idea that I had a genetically related
weakness in math just because I found it challenging. I had
never credited myself with having solved and even enjoyed
some of the puzzles of algebra and geometry. When an aptitude test in junior high school had indicated that I possessed
some aptitude for engineering, I assumed that the test had
made a mistake.

I began connecting with deep layers within myself including a longstanding fascination with science, especially
human biology, which I had not pursued because I had not
seen any career possibilities as a woman. Due to the women's
movement, though, my attitude was changing, and I thought,
*Maybe, just maybe, it's not too late to pursue this buried yearn-
ing.* I did pursue that yearning, and the forthcoming years
were a challenge but nothing like the previous years of inde-
cision, guilt, and depression.

Chapter 11

LISTENING TO GOD, GODDESSES, DEVILS, AND EVERYONE ELSE

By the early 1970s, I was traveling along five different tracks: caring for three children; protesting the war; participating in the women's movement; studying for challenging classes in chemistry, biology, and physics; and simultaneously becoming more and more addicted to marijuana. What was I thinking? Well, I was thinking a lot! Around and around in my head, I went. What to do?

Subsequently studying and writing a master's thesis in public health was stressful enough, but I was also becoming acutely sensitive to noise. I escaped into the backyard and watched our home pulsating with the purple light of the TV, booming music from the stereo, and the voices of my sons and husband getting louder and louder as everyone tried to shout over the background noise.

My husband initially supported me in my school and anti-war and feminist efforts, and I didn't personally blame him for my current frustrations. Yet my constant going to meetings and protests and arguing about responsibilities for cooking, cleaning, and childcare put an understandable strain on our relationship.

Along with my frustrations with rigid gender roles was a questioning of the assumed righteousness of monogamy. This questioning had its roots in my childhood, when I had observed the unfair isolation of my mother, while my father spent nine years in a hospital with TB. Although my mother was married, she had none of the love, support, or sex of an actual marriage. She was a widow while her husband was alive. One time I had asked her why she never went to any of the neighborhood parties. She replied that the other married women in those gatherings would feel threatened by a woman there without a husband.

Single women of the 1950s were either "old maids" to be pitied or potential threats to marriages. They certainly didn't have any of the rights to sex or even the companionship of other women's husbands. In my mind, monogamy was linked with selfishness. Why couldn't women share husbands when there was a shortage of men? And vice versa? Or if there was no shortage but someone was sick and his or her spouse needed support? Although monogamy appeared to be valuable for providing stability and avoiding jealousy, no one seemed to acknowledge its limitations.

"You never get what you want," said my yoga teacher, who was well versed in Hindu philosophy. "You never get what you want because as soon as you get what you want, your desire, which is the root of your being, simply switches on to something else." I think that must have been true, because first I had wished to be married and have children, but eighteen years later, I was wishing to be unmarried without children. Not really without children just without the constant responsibility and frustration. Why was I frustrated? I was frustrated because it seemed that despite constantly loving and caring for our three children, I couldn't seem to keep up. I was always behind on cooking, cleaning, and resolving temper tantrums and fights.

It wasn't just my husband and children who felt like they were pulling my psyche in a myriad of different ways; it was also my mother. I loved my mother, but she had her own problems, including not only the typical problems of aging but also a physical weakness I attributed to the feminine dictates of those times. The feminine high heels and narrow shoes she wore created chronic bunions and corns, which the chiropodist always had to cut off. The big toe on one foot had been so squeezed that one day it simply collapsed horizontally below her other toes. Walking, her only exercise, became excruciatingly painful.

My mother also had a deep-seated unhappiness, which I saw as related to her decade of being married but not married, which had led to a distrust of all men. She was prone to insomnia, which I have also experienced, but her medically advised remedies of alcohol and sleeping pills created other problems. Tension and depression combined with alcohol and nicotine dependence were powerful forces I wasn't equipped to understand at the time. Only in later decades, when introduced to the concepts of Alcoholic Anonymous, did I realize how nicotine and alcohol had played havoc with the lives of my parents, me, and at least one of our children.

One night I had a dream that I was laid out on a dining table and being carved up by a crowd of people with different needs. On another night, I had a dream, in which I was a passenger on a boat in the middle of the ocean. The boat was sinking, and all the passengers were grabbing onto me for safety. I felt panic as we all sank to the bottom of the sea, but suddenly I had a thought. *Perhaps this is a dream. If it is a dream, I can change it.* I then asked the ocean floor to rise, the water drained off, and we all walked out into a beautiful sunset over clear, blue shallow water.

I couldn't leave my husband and children, whom I loved, but I couldn't stay in my current role, and I couldn't handle the constant noise. Simultaneously, I was also becoming aware of how I must appear to them. I felt I was becoming sick and that I would be doing everyone a favor if I simply took myself out of the picture.

It sounds like this would have been a fitting time to seek professional counseling, but I didn't. And why was that? My first reason was that professional counseling would cost money, which I didn't have since I had never felt like the money earned by my husband was partly my money. Of course, I was spending some of that same money to go to school, but classes at that time were much less expensive than any kind of professional counseling. Second, most psychologists and psychiatrists in the 1970s were men, and I was under no illusions that they would understand, much less be sympathetic to or have practical suggestions to address my frustrations.

Hiring a professional housekeeper would have been a practical solution to the constant cleaning need, which was draining my energy, but that would have conflicted with my deeply felt ideals about being an equalitarian, non-racist, and non-classist kind of person. I simply couldn't imagine hiring a black or brown or even white woman so I could be liberated from my stereotype while perpetuating what I saw as the oppressive stereotype of another woman.

Round and round I went. I prayed (even though I was an atheist) but saw only a wall, behind which I stayed and made the best of the situation I had, after all, helped to create and build. Simultaneously, God or my better angel (or was it the devil in me?) was also proposing that I would be cowardly not to pursue a life on my own. I fantasized about buying a bus ticket to somewhere like Brazil. As a true American, individual freedom was the highest goal. Right? We all needed freedom. It had always been a dream for me and our children, yet it was probably responsible for much of the chaos in our household. One of my most impractical fantasies was that my husband would fall in love and marry another woman, who would step into my role and free us all.

No one, least of all me, could have blamed my husband for beginning to look for love elsewhere. Besides, I, myself, was tempted to have affairs—not that I was seeking love, just the curiosity and excitement of romance and sex with another man. And then in an amazingly short time, after about two years, my fantasy of another woman rescuing us both began to come to life. We talked things over, hired the same lawyer, and agreed upon living arrangements and how to divide up the financial assets (one house, two cars, pension plans, and a $3,000 cash settlement). The court decree ratified our agreement so he and the children could remain in the home and I could move into my fantasy of a small apartment. The decree included provisions that I would pay one-third of the estimated child support with an equivalent tax deduction and that the children would visit me on certain weekends and holidays.

On the morning of the chosen day, I took my mother to the airport, where she boarded a plane to El Paso (the city of my brother and his wife). As I drove away from the airport, the rain stopped, and I watched as clear, blue skies appeared behind silvery clouds. I took this to be a sign of a new life to come. (It was a bit arrogant of me to think that the sky would rearrange itself for one person among all the billions of people and animals on the planet, but I enjoyed the feeling.) That evening we all went to see our eldest son perform a cheese-selling routine at the Houston Livestock Show, and I then left to spend the first night by myself in my new apartment. I rested.

Chapter 12

RESHAPING A FAMILY

My move into a separate apartment was the start of striving to be separate while still connected to my now-former husband and our children. This was more challenging than I had naively expected. My plans had included having one child at a time come to live with me for about six months so I could build a more meaningful relationship with each one without the competition of two other siblings. Nice idea, but it wasn't to be since not one of them accepted my invitation. I felt hurt but also understood that, after all, I was the one who had moved out. Everyone else simply stayed where he was.

We signed a "no fault" divorce in October of 1979. Several members of our respective families were surprised and mystified when it happened. This was likely because we had never visibly fought or complained about each other. In truth, I still loved him and our children and I believe he still cared for me.

There were conflicting feelings about the divorce. Underlying my need to leave was a fear that I would never be able to break out of the assumption that I would always be the one to cook and clean up. The unacknowledged economic value of homemakers (the older term was "housewives") also challenged me to see if I could support myself and some of the children as a measure of self-respect. That fear and drive plus my growing needs for quiet and solitude just exerted too strong a pull.

My husband remarried within a few months and seemed relaxed and happy. The reactions of our children seemed muted and varied. Our oldest son appeared to take it all in stride as he continued with his busy life in high school with a part-time job in a retail cheese store, numerous friends, and various events. My second son was having outbursts of anger, but these seemed to be at about the same rate as he had always had them. He and I had a few awkward conversations, and I repeatedly invited him to visit me in my apartment, which was only a short distance away. However, he seemed resistant and often said he was busy with his friends and other events. Our youngest son, who was twelve at the time, said he missed me and would even "make a place for me in his room" if I would come back. That invitation almost broke my heart, but there was no turning back. I then simply made a point of showing up consistently and inviting whoever was available and interested to go out to dinner or a movie, or to take a trip such as camping or going to the beach.

Gratefully, that first Thanksgiving was celebrated together in our previous home thanks to the combined invitation from

my former husband and his new wife. We subsequently celebrated numerous combined holidays together. Rather than
feeling any resentment or jealousy, I appreciated that my
husband's new wife had relieved me of many of my previous responsibilities. It was not just the responsibilities, but
rather, what I felt like was my declining effectiveness. I believe
my sons even benefitted from the perspectives of another
woman in the role of mother.

The following decades were filled with many adventures
and new relationships for both me and my husband's newly
formed family. I met someone who became a love companion
and grew close to his former wife and their daughter. During
the next five years, he and I enjoyed both of our families and
friends, and we took a bicycle trip through northern Germany,
Denmark, and Sweden. Sadly, he was diagnosed with untreat-
able lung cancer, and ten months later, worn out from the
pain, he committed suicide.

About a year later, I married my second husband, whom
I had met on a bike ride from Houston to Austin, and I grew
close to his three adult children. Unexpectedly, he also died
five years later from a squamous cell sarcoma skin cancer.
Meanwhile, I continued to support myself through two different careers—cancer research and massage therapy.

Although the family of my first husband and I had divided,
we kept in contact, and the family didn't end; it simply regrew
in new directions. The next decades were ones in which our
three sons began their own adult lives and formed families,
but those would be their stories to tell.

Part Four

EATING, DRINKING, AND BREATHING

Chapter 13

SWINGING BETWEEN
NUTRITION CONCEPTS

Lessons about foods during my lifetime have felt like a series of swinging from one pole to another of authoritative teachings. When I was a child in the 1940s, the fat on meat was considered good for me. I thought it was yucky and carefully cut it away. Once at Sunday dinner, my grandmother insisted that I eat it. I tried my best, but it made me gag, almost ejecting it onto the table; so that was the end of that. By the 1980s, we were hearing about the dangers of animal fats and the benefits of vegetable oils. I then avoided not only the fats in meat but also the fats of any dairy products. I added vegetable oils to my diet, but I lost a lot of weight, so much so that my skin sagged, and my lips dried out. Apparently, my body couldn't utilize those vegetable oils as efficiently as the dairy fats.

As a child, I enjoyed all kinds of lean meat, milk, vegetables, salads, fruits, candy, and ice cream; however, I broke out in a rash after eating any kind of white bread, cake, or cookies. This reaction had stopped by the time I was in junior high school; I don't know why. After I went away to college, however, the problem mysteriously returned in the form of scaly, itchy patches on the same fingers of both hands, in circles under my eyes, and on one side of my mouth. Of course, I went to general doctors and dermatologists, who prescribed various salves and advised me to wear rubber gloves when washing dishes. (All dish washing was by hand in those days.) I did as they advised, but the rashes continued. At times they abated but never fully disappeared.

Then when I became pregnant with our first child, I read a book called *How to Have Healthy Children*,[8] which emphasized the value of eating whole grains whether in cereals or breads. I immediately began buying whole wheat breads. The rashes disappeared. Was it due to the breads and cereal, or could it have been due to the pregnancy? All I know is that the rashes never came back. Decades later, a gastroenterologist said that probably my eosinophil cells had simply become less sensitive. I suppose that's possible, but I still find the timing to be too much of a coincidence. There was something either in the white bread or lacking in it associated with those miserable rashes.

I ate lots of meat as a child and through three pregnancies. Meat tasted good and was said to be "good for you." This was in the days when vegetarians were extremely rare, although they were said to be common in India. I glibly rationalized the killing of animals as necessary for survival without thinking too much about it.

Following the births and breastfeeding of three babies, however, I was having health issues—mainly, chronic fatigue. I began searching for answers in what I was eating. Everything I read encouraged increased intake of protein, especially meat and eggs and a decrease of caffeine, sugars, and starches. Since my husband's family owned a ranch, I was already eating a lot of meat, but I began to eat even more. I stopped (well, almost stopped) the caffeine and sugar. No matter how much protein I ate, though, my cravings for sugar and caffeine continued and seemed to be getting worse.

Still in search of relief from my continued fatigue, which had progressed to episodes of feeling like I was about to pass out, I began jogging and playing tennis against a backboard. Still, the fatigue continued. Then I tried Yoga, a challenge for my chronically tight muscles, but it felt like it was what I needed. One day, my Yoga teacher talked about the horror of killing animals and the health benefits of vegetarianism. *Hmm*, I thought. *I couldn't feel any worse than I do now, so I might as well try to give up eating meat.* This was shortly after I had had the experience of driving past a huge cattle feedlot in West Texas. The smell of animals and manure had never bothered me, but that smell was different. It smelled of vomit, which caused me to question the whole meat industry.

I stopped eating meat and found that I didn't miss it. I also began reading the recently published book *Diet for a Small Planet*.[9] The author presented an analysis of the amino acids in eggs, meat, milk, beans, corn, and other grains. She presented eggs as the perfect protein since they contained all the amino acids in perfect balance, followed by meats and dairy.

She then described the amino acid beans lacked—which was found in whole grains. Thus, she said, one could get all the necessary amino acids by eating combinations of beans and whole grains. I began to follow this pattern, and by the end of two weeks, I realized I was feeling not just okay but full of energy. The biggest surprise was that I no longer craved sugar. I did well for several years with whole grains, beans, vegetables, fruits, eggs, and milk. Although I occasionally enjoyed sweets, I no longer craved them.

In 1982, about four years after becoming a vegetarian, I went on a bicycle tour in China and had three weeks of eating authentic Chinese meals. I had heard that Chinese cuisine would be largely vegetarian with only small amounts of meat served as a garnish. To the surprise of all of us in our group, meat was served at every meal and in more than small amounts. Nevertheless, I ate it since I had decided to experience everything fully as a guest in this different culture. What wasn't served was either coffee or any kind of dairy food. Going without coffee didn't bother me, since I was mainly a tea drinker, and I only slightly missed the dairy. Unexpectedly, about halfway through the trip, everyone else in our group and I realized we had lost our body odor. We all compared notes and agreed that it must have been the absence of dairy products.

Upon my return from China, I thought more about that unexpected connection between dairy products and body odor, and I decided to drop milk from my diet. One day a friend talked me into attending a lecture about an adaptation of Eastern food theories, known as "macrobiotics." By this time, I was bored with constantly thinking about food and its preparation, but the speaker made so much sense that I was immediately hooked.

The theories of macrobiotics were based on the philosophy of opposites known as yin and yang; for example, up and down, in and out, light and dark, and so forth. Macrobiotic teachers applied this philosophy to a spectrum of foods based on their characteristic of density. They proposed that the densest foods were meat, eggs, and hard cheeses; while the least dense were fruits, pastries, and alcohol. Whole grains, cooked beans, and vegetables were situated in the center of that spectrum. They further proposed that if a person ate most of his or her food on one end of the spectrum of density, it would lead to cravings for foods on the opposite end of the spectrum.[10]

Suddenly, a light bulb went off in my mind; I recalled my previous eating of more and more protein and my growing craving for sugar and alcohol. I also recalled many times when I had diligently provided healthy meals of meat and vegetables, while my children begged for cookies and candy.

For the next eight years, I expanded my vegetarianism to include macrobiotic concepts so my diet became centered on beans, whole grains, and vegetables with the addition of seaweeds. As with most Asian cuisines, there were no dairy products. For the first few years, everything went well; I felt healthy and had lots of energy. However, I began losing weight and continued losing weight. Most people who began eating macrobiotically were delighted to be losing weight, but I wasn't since I hadn't been overweight. I lost so much weight that my ribs stuck out, and my skin sagged. I awoke at two or three a.m. with such strong cravings for ice cream that I walked to the nearest all-night store.

Once during my abstinence from dairy products, I ended a twenty-four-hour fast with a glass a soy drink. My stomach immediately became nauseous. *Hmmm*, I thought, *cow milk has never made me feel nauseous*. Then I read an article about northern Europeans surviving on the meat and milk of herd animals during the ice ages and subsequent winters.[11] It seemed to me that something of my ancestors' adaptation to life must have been preserved in my DNA.

I also realized I was now having the same episodes of loss of energy I had previously had when eating meat. Apparently, the theory of density spectrum eating wasn't complete if one omitted meat as those of us who were vegetarians had done. Then I accepted the reality that, regardless of various vegetarian and non-dairy theories, I wasn't doing well at five feet four inches in height and now weighing only ninety-nine pounds. I reintroduced meat (including fish) and dairy, and I slowly began regaining my weight, energy, and a healthier appearance. In the three decades since then, I have done well as an omnivore, but I know others who are doing well as vegetarians.

Chapter 14

THE LAST TIMES I GOT DRUNK (OR EVEN A LITTLE TIPSY)

"A loaf of bread, a jug of wine and thou."[12] What could be more perfect? The same plus a gorgeous sunny day in the Rocky Mountains with your husband, three children, and two friends. To top it all off, we were listening to Doc Watson play the guitar for a crowd of young people in love with it all. The music thrilled my ears, and my feet itched to move with the rhythms. Like everyone else in that crowd of about a thousand, however, I was too shy to be the first to stand and maybe even the only one to dance. But I had to dance! Then I thought, *If I drink just a little more wine, I won't care what other people think.* I drank a little more and then a little more, and soon I was dancing and dancing and loving it.

I remained, however, the lone dancer amid a crowd of about a thousand apparently healthy young people, who just sat and twitched in time to the music. With no other dancers to keep me company, I simply danced with my shadow while feeling the joy of all my ancestral Irish dancers. Gradually the music ended, and we all began leaving, but suddenly the earth began tilting under my feet, and it was a struggle to keep upright. I barely made it to the car with my family while fighting dizziness, nausea, and the most incredible thirst I had ever experienced. That night was one of the longest of my life with an aching head, no sleep, and unending thirst. The next morning, I concluded, *Alcohol isn't worth it. Next time, I won't care about my own shyness and what other people think. I'll just dance!*

I had no intention of giving up alcohol entirely; only my need to drink to overcome shyness. I still enjoyed its taste. Alcohol can be tricky, though, and the next time I drank, it fooled me. I had joined a group of fellow workers out on the lawn after work on a Friday evening. We enjoyed a few snacks, a beer or two, and some interesting conversations and joking. I had had only two beers when we said our goodbyes, and I drove a short way to join my other friends … the ones who had gathered to folk dance—no beer, no wine, no food—just dancing.

I did a few easy line dances, and then someone grabbed my hand for a Hungarian dance. Hungarians, at least at that time, were famous for their spinning dances. That's spinning fast while whirling around the floor. And I began spinning and loving it. And then the room began spinning. When the dance ended, it took incredible, miraculous effort for me to remain upright while walking to the nearest chair with the room still spinning. That was my second lesson in alcohol … two beers drunk slowly with food aren't that much, unless followed by dancing, especially vigorous dancing and most especially any spinning dances. So, because I loved to dance and especially loved spinning dances, any alcohol before dancing had to go.

Chapter 15

STRANGE WEED

The first time I tried marijuana, I developed a painful crick in my neck due to constantly looking over my shoulder, where I was sure the police, the FBI, the neighbors, my mother, and my conscience were watching me. The next time I smoked it, I literally felt like I was higher than my body. *Wow*, I thought, *that's why they call it "high,"* and *I can exist beyond my own body.*

Yet I also felt conflicted because I was now sucking smoke into my lungs, which violated my deep conviction about protecting my health. Having grown up with two chain-smoking parents and suffering from related colds, sore throats, and coughs during my childhood and teen years, I found the habit to be both dangerous and disgusting. Yet I was intrigued by the feelings occurring with marijuana, unlike those reported by tobacco smokers, which seemed to be simply desperate pleadings that they "needed a cigarette."

Marijuana seemed to awaken my senses, slow down time, and sharpen my ability to focus. The taste of an orange became the essence of an orange and awakened childhood experiences of oranges. Music became not only enjoyable but also incredible—reaching into deep parts of my mind and soul. I saw its patterns clearly for the first time. Colors became more intense, and nature became more alive.

At first, I rarely smoked marijuana and only with a few trusted friends, since it was both against the law and frightening to most people. When someone scored a hit during a trip to Mexico, found it growing wild in Oklahoma or Texas, or grew their own, they shared it with their close friends. Rolling a joint or lighting a corncob pipe and then passing it around was a warm and friendly occasion.

Feelings of mischievousness led to inside jokes and nicknames: *weed, grass* (which it smelled like when burned), *pot, joint, stoned.* The sensations heightened by marijuana included our gratitude for being within a small circle of trusted friends. Our conversations ranged from interesting and wise to funny or just silly. Within our stoned conversations, I found myself watching my thoughts and realizing they were both worthwhile and needing to be expressed.

One evening I suddenly felt an almost-spiritual connection to the tales of Native Americans passing around the peace pipe. Were they smoking marijuana? Tobacco? Some other weed? I believe it could have been any of these plants, but it would have been different from contemporary smoking of tobacco. A century or more in the past, any of these plants would have been harvested only during one season of the year and only in a few places. Smoking a limited substance within a small and trusted circle of friends would have been an entirely different experience from smoking it all day long every day by oneself.

As more and more small circles of friends began smoking pot, a terrifying backdrop was growing—the war in Vietnam. That war, which no one understood, simply heightened our feelings that the world outside was a strange and frightening place in contrast to our own feelings of peace and serenity. We even began to believe that if more people smoked marijuana, there would be peace in the world.

I continued to smoke marijuana for decades, although never while pregnant or nursing. Slowly over the years, I switched from smoking only in a small group to smoking at other times. I smoked before going to a movie or dancing or during the day when I was bored or frustrated or tired.

Once when I was overwhelmed by the chaos of toys and other objects strewn across my recently vacuumed living room, I slipped into the bathroom and smoked a joint. Upon emerging, I saw the chaos as something new—a beautiful train that had been artistically constructed by my clever children. This refreshing insight expanded my pattern to smoking when I needed to access parental insights.

Meanwhile, I was developing recurring and worsening bouts of depression, which could be alleviated only with marijuana, which became less and less effective. I finally had enough insight to realize I was on a downward spiral between marijuana and depression. I tried to manage this by limiting the times I smoked, but there were always exceptions that would disrupt the plan—someone had just arrived for a visit, or there was a special batch from somewhere, or I needed insight about a certain problem.

Then I realized I just had to stop, period. I stopped, and although the depression remained, it wasn't any worse. I also realized that part of the attraction of smoking weed was simply the long, deep breaths, and I replaced those with the structured breathing of yoga.

Still, I missed the early excitement of smoking weed, and life no longer appeared to have its previous peacefulness, intensity, or sparkle. I just kept going, though, one foot in front of the other (a lesson I had learned decades before in a movie about soldiers struggling out of a jungle).

One day I was walking outside when it began to rain. I unfurled my umbrella, congratulated myself on having had the foresight to bring it, and continued walking. As I walked along, I began to appreciate the sensation of being warm and dry under my umbrella. I also realized that sunlight was shining through the raindrops so they sparkled. Then it hit me. *The sparkle is back*! And it *was* back; I was alive again and able to see the sparkle in life with my own eyes and mind; all I had to do was pay attention.

That return of sparkle to my life should have been enough for me to know I didn't need marijuana, but it wasn't. I resumed the habit years later while having a love affair with someone else, who smoked marijuana. Then one day, I coughed up bright-red blood, which finally got my attention. I concluded that whatever the value of marijuana was, it wasn't worth the price of my lungs, and I dropped the habit completely. As with my previous lesson about alcohol, I was also helped by my competing love of folk dancing, which required full attention and coordination incompatible with being stoned.

Decades later, I tried marijuana sautéed in oil on toast and then began writing. Rather than finding that my focus was enhanced, however; I found myself rewriting and wandering through the same sentence over and over. I realized that it had interrupted my own matured focus. A few years after that, I ate it in a brownie prepared by a friend and carefully arranged my setting to be out of doors by myself with no tasks. This time, I felt that I did, indeed, experience a heightened focus on the sounds of the wind, shapes of clouds and clarity of my thoughts. Although I valued these insights, I also recognized that whatever value Marijuana had added would only continue for me if this indulgence remained a rare event (once or twice a year). If I once again became habituated to its frequent use, I would risk losing my own innate abilities to appreciate sights, sounds, and clear thoughts.

Part Five

MY HEALTH AND THEIRS

Chapter 16

HEALTH RESEARCH COUNTS

After receiving my degree in history and a couple of short-lived teaching jobs, I found myself more and more questioning my choice of teaching as a career. Before the women's movement of the 1960s, it had simply been one of only three careers open to women: teaching, nursing, and secretarial work. Yet the new life unfolding in my body during three pregnancies had awakened an underlying fascination with biology. This initiated a frustrating mental and emotional struggle between the allure of a career in science, for which I wasn't prepared, and guilt for the time and money previously invested in preparing me for a career in teaching history.

My long mental struggle was finally resolved one day when I imagined myself years in the future standing in front of a classroom of young students. I saw myself resenting those students because they were going to pursue the careers that I had wanted to pursue but hadn't done. *No,* I thought. *I can't do that. I must start on a path that reflects who I am, even if the path is long, costly, and difficult—and even if I fail. I, at least, must start on my path.* Amazingly, the instant I had that thought, I had the unmistakable feeling of a physical weight sliding off my shoulders. Yes, the path was long, costly, and difficult, but not nearly as difficult as it would have been if I had continued to struggle with guilt and depression.

My first task on this new path was to develop some grounding in science beyond what I had previously learned and mostly forgotten from over a decade ago. I began with a course in chemistry, and, feeling like an imposter, I walked into a large class of students, fresh out of high school. Although I tried my best to listen closely to the lectures and study, I failed the first test. I then realized that although I had diligently memorized the name of the scientist and year in which a pattern of X-rays had revealed the existence of atomic particles, I had skipped over the subsequent equations since I figured those were just examples of what *real* scientists did. In other words, I had studied as if it were a history test and not a chemistry test.

I had never previously failed any kind of test, so this was a shock, yet it was an effective lesson that changed my method of studying. I managed to pass the remaining tests and earn a C for the semester. Changing from one who had always been an A or B student to one who was now a C student was a lesson in humility. I now saw all those C students I had previously looked down on in a new light.

After two years of chemistry, biology, physics, remedial algebra, and calculus, I applied to the master's degree program at the University of Texas School of Public Health. You, the reader, must be wondering how my husband and I were able to afford this continued schooling without my having a paying job. Three factors made this possible: first, at that time the local university wasn't that expensive—something like a hundred dollars per semester. Second, my husband, like many men at that time, made enough money to cover the cost of a wife who didn't have a paying job. Third, we were both financially conservative, buying used furniture and holding off on purchases of appliances until we could pay cash. I was now simply spending money on school rather than on new clothes. Although I will always be grateful for what his salary allowed me to do, I will also never forget the guilt and resentment I felt because my own work of cooking, cleaning, and caring for children wasn't considered worthy of separate compensation or even recognized as work.

On the first day of the graduate school in public health, I learned a new word—*epidemiology*, the study of epidemics. How do you know an epidemic has begun? How do you know whether it has ended or is at least decreasing? How do you find out what can be done to either prevent it or end it?

I was introduced to this fascinating field through the story of John Snow (1813–1858), a physician practicing in London during the cholera outbreak of 1854. Frustrated by the lack of a treatment, he focused on who was getting the disease. He took detailed notes about all his patients: their addresses, ages, genders, when they had become sick, and what they had recently eaten or drunk. He then inquired as to who else had the disease and searched through the records of all deaths in London. He noted cases on a map along with locations of rivers and water pumps and found that, with one exception, those with cholera lived in a neighborhood that used the same water pump. The one exception was someone who lived outside the neighborhood but had bought medicine from an herbalist living in the neighborhood.

He then turned his attention to those in the neighborhood who hadn't been sick and learned they were all men employed by or routinely drinking beer in the local brewery. He didn't know what was in the water or what had protected the beer drinkers, but he knew something in the water was killing people. He presented his findings to Queen Victoria, who ordered that a lock be placed on the pump, and the epidemic ended. It sounds simple, but further details of his story indicate that he had years of frustration, in which other physicians and authorities wouldn't accept his findings.[13,14]

The word *research* had always fascinated me, and this story of the water pump showed me the possibilities of research outside of laboratories. Full of enthusiasm, I began preparing a master's thesis with questions based on my own recent experiences with pregnancy and breast feeding. I was convinced that breast feeding was the healthiest way to feed infants simply because that was how our female breasts appeared to be designed. I didn't know, though, whether any benefits had been scientifically demonstrated.

After immersing myself in medical journals, I found that, indeed, the benefits of human milk had been well investigated

and reported. I summarized the laboratory and human studies for the first part of my master's thesis, but I also wanted
to know why more women weren't currently breastfeeding.
Most people I talked to immediately said it was because
women were working, but I suspected there were additional
reasons. To further explore these reasons, I interviewed a hundred pregnant women in five of the public health clinics in
Houston. I asked the study participants whether they were
planning on breastfeeding or bottle feeding and what had
influenced their choices. As anticipated, many of them had
chosen bottle feeding because of jobs outside the home, but
others had based their choices on wanting to be "scientific"
because they had read the ingredients of baby formulas on
the labels or because they hadn't heard breastfeeding mentioned by their obstetricians. Some even feared that their husbands would be jealous.

Because my project occurred before the availability of
personal computers, I had to compile the necessary statistics by counting and recounting innumerable stacks of cards,
in which I had recorded my interviews. I learned an important lesson when I found out how many copying, counting,
and arithmetic errors I had made despite my careful efforts.
Sophisticated statistical analysis is worthless if there are
counting errors. Everyone needs someone or some machine
to check his or her work.

Looking for a job after receiving my master's degree was
more difficult than studying for the degree. My passion for
studying childbirth and breastfeeding based on my own
experiences didn't count in a field that required an official

nursing degree. After completing numerous applications with no resulting job offers, I became more and more depressed. Finally, I was offered a job as an administrative assistant based largely on my knowing how to type. Although everyone knows how to type today, this wasn't true before the advent of computers. At that time, typing was something women did. Men dictated their words to secretaries, who were almost entirely women, who took notes by hand and then typed them.

I struggled with whether to accept a job that wasn't based on my background in science or to continue at home frustrated, depressed and not feeling like I was being an effective mother. Then I considered a recently learned concept concerning research.

Clinical trials assign participants to different treatments or a placebo in ways that attempt to avoid either conscious or unconscious bias. Biased assignments, for example, would happen if those who are younger were disproportionately placed in one group rather than another. To avoid bias, assignment to treatment groups is determined by random processes such as computer-generated random numbers or even the simple act of tossing a coin. *Ah-ha*, I thought, *since I have already considered all pros and cons of my two possibilities and still don't know what to do, I need a random process to guide the decision.*

It occurred to me that if something as critical to life as treatment or no treatment could be determined by a coin toss, I could let a coin toss influence the next step in my own life. I also decided that if I was going to toss a coin, I needed to do it in a grand way. I recalled that I had recently been given a copy of *The I Ching or Book of Changes*,[15] a book of wisdom based on patterns of coin tosses. I followed that book's complex instructions for nine different coin tosses, which led to a proverb, which stated, "To proceed forward could invite disaster; to remain behind danger."

That simple statement perfectly encapsulated my position and helped me to decide. I knew that going forward by accepting the job offer could be a disaster, but I also knew my current mental and emotional state was dangerous. I believed it would be better for me to face and handle whatever disaster lay in the future than for me to continue in my current mental and emotional state.

I began my new job, anxious to do it well, but still conflicted and fighting off a new source of guilt for letting down all those other women who were trying to avoid automatic assignment to typewriters. In addition, I found myself working for a doctor who had a lot of anger expressed quite freely and often inappropriately. I told myself, though, that these factors were part of the disaster alluded to by the *I Ching* and vowed to deal with it as best I could. To my surprise, I began to recognize certain gifts in the job as I realized my somewhat lowly job status allowed me access to the memos and files of the most powerful figures within the hospital.

My first task was to compile a list of all patients receiving radiation within different clinical trials, then to send letters to the appropriate radiation oncologists requesting X-rays and radiation summaries. The purpose was so a physicist could determine whether their radiation treatment had been within the specifications of the clinical trial protocol. This process was extremely tedious, but I could see its importance. To relieve the tediousness and increase its efficiency, I took it on myself to design a computer program for tracking the records.

Designing a record-tracking system would be a no-brainer today, but at that time, computerized tracking systems weren't common. A new one required designing your own program with a set of logic pathways for each record. "If this, do that; if the other, do something else," and so forth. It was so mentally challenging that at times my head hurt. Nevertheless, I pursued, and thanks to the help of my husband, who was an experienced programmer, I eventually had a logical and smoothly running data-tracking system. I briefly enjoyed my success but then found that entering the data was extremely tedious. *Gee*, I thought, *I have used my intellect to design another set of boring tasks for myself.*

Although I received recognition and appreciation for my tracking system, the grant that paid my salary wasn't renewed due to disagreements between the doctor for whom I was working and other members of the cooperative research group. This was a lesson in which I was simply the witness and the victim. In truth, I was a bit relieved because I now felt free to seek another job. This time, however, I had valuable experience under my belt and the beginnings of a solid work reputation.

My next job was in the department that managed the hospital's patient registry database stored within a large computer, known as the mainframe. That computer and its auxiliary components took up the entire floor of one building.

Today it would probably fit within a cell phone! My new job was to identify subgroups of patients within the database, provide a report of their characteristics (age, ethnicity, sex, type of cancer, registration at the hospital, admission for a specific type of cancer, cancer-specific treatments, status when last contacted, and more). This was less tedious than previous work, since a commercial software package was now available for analyses and printed reports.

In a short while, though, I learned some disquieting information. A coworker showed me that the neatly printed computer table of total alive and dead didn't agree with the survival analysis produced by the same program. How could that be? No one seemed to have any idea other than "There must be something wrong with the data." Or "It's only a small miscount anyway." This response offended my faith in computers and logic. *Well*, I thought, *I still know how to count, so I will set up some imaginary data and compare my manual counting to the computer report.*

I wrote down the admission and last dates seen or death dates of some imaginary patients into a writing pad and manually summed up their months of survival. I then entered those same dates into a computer file and used the commercial software package to analyze their survival. The resulting computer analysis immediately revealed a discrepancy that occurred only among patients who had a date of last contact within the first month. This discrepancy had occurred because the computer had classified these patients as dead due to their zero months of survival, while my manual count had counted them as unknown status but as having survived on average at least halfway through the first month.

After a flurry of memos between departments, it was acknowledged that an error had been embedded within this large commercial software package, which was in use all over the world. It was subsequently corrected and provided me with a dramatic lesson in not assuming that the neatly printed computer report would always be right.

I had numerous subsequent lessons in questioning both the analysis and the sources and quality of data. One time I noticed that many people appeared to be counting and generating handwritten lists of names to be typed by a secretary. When I asked the source of those names, I found it was a computer printout. This seemed like a terrible waste of time, so I set about learning why it was happening. I followed the source of data on the list from one department to another until I had followed a complete circle involving at least four different departments—back to my own department. A description of the process, another set of memos to various departments, and that circular process ended.

Is a medicine or other treatment effective? What do you mean by "effective"? Are people cured? What does "cured" mean? Will this treatment save lives? What does that mean? Everyone dies eventually; the only question is when. All these questions require definitions and a collection of information (data) and counting, lots of counting. Only then can one begin to summarize and then finally analyze differences and similarities between groups and subgroups.

Even with powerful computer processing, the process still

requires many layers of knowledgeable and conscientious people to define questions, collect and input data, check for errors and inconsistencies, thoughtfully consider initial analysis, and collaborate with others such as statisticians on subsequent analysis. Summarizing reams of data into digestible reports for publication requires additional collaboration and further reviews by independent reviewers. It's an intensive and fascinating labor, which requires patience, perseverance, and lots of counting.

Chapter 17

A FALL LEADS ME ON
TO A NEW PATH

Early in my twenties, I had noticed something strange about my right shoulder; it protruded in front of the rest of my body. I could force it back in line, but as soon as I relaxed, it popped forward. I didn't know why it protruded forward; perhaps it had been my decades of right-handedness. It didn't seem like a big deal until the day I fell down ice skating, and its forward position absorbed most of the force. Over the next few weeks, my shoulder hurt so much that I couldn't sleep.

I went to an orthopedic specialist, who ordered X-rays and then pronounced that nothing was broken. But something *was* broken. Decades later, after the invention of MRIs, I learned that two tendons had been torn. By then they had retracted back to their origins, so they were no longer repairable. Physical therapy instructions to "walk my fingers up the

wall" produced excruciating pain, so I stopped. I was determined to keep active, even returning to occasional tennis
volleys against a wall, but the pain was always there.

Then I began hearing about the benefits of massage and
paid for a series of sessions. Although these didn't cure my
chronic shoulder pain, they helped my overall body, which
had begun to bend and tighten in response to my painful
shoulder. In the process, I began to wonder whether I might
learn how to do massage.

Learning massage appealed to me for several reasons.
Ever since my three pregnancies, I had become more and
more fascinated by the human body and saw massage as an
opportunity for more in-depth learning. In addition to my
chronically painful shoulder, my back had been complaining
after long days of sitting at a computer, and I was chafing under the feudal dictatorship of our department chairperson. I
was also weary of the many survival analyses, in which I spent
days counting people with the aid of a computer. Although
my job was interesting and paid me a reasonable salary, I felt
that I was somehow off track and simply counting bodies
rather than helping anyone to either prevent or heal from
sickness.

I saw great potential in massage for relieving the tension
and pain in my own and other peoples' bodies. *At least, even
if I am not able to cure anyone of anything*, I thought, *I can help
them feel better for a time. I will also be helping myself by doing
less sitting, being more physically active, and managing my own
business.*

I began to study anatomy and the practice of massage

in weekly nighttime classes and obtained Texas state certi-fication about a year later. Although some of my teachers also seemed to be beginners, others were highly experienced and imparted in-depth knowledge and ways to sense what was happening in clients' bodies. I resigned from my job and cashed out what had accumulated in a retirement account at the very time my back had had enough and was giving me bouts of excruciating pain.

During my first few months free of the confines of a full-time job, I rested and worked on my back problems through a series of Pilates exercises and other therapies. I went to a month-long intensive massage training course in Toronto, Canada, and then returned to plunge into having my own small business in massage. Over the next decade, I continued to attend workshops in various types of massage and mas-saged many different people. Slowly I found that my own hands were becoming more and more adept at feeling what was happening in other people's bodies.

What I hadn't expected to learn concerned the economics of having a small business. I had thought that all I had to do was become skilled at doing massage, and word of mouth would then bring a steady stream of customers to my door. Although I had cashed out my pension to fund the starting years of the business, I saw how rapidly it was dwindling while I waited for my skills to deepen and the word to spread. I now recognized that spreading the word wasn't working—at least, not fast enough.

Remaining in business was going to require something that had always annoyed me—paid advertising. Soon enough,

I found a small widely circulated newspaper with classified ads that weren't too expensive and applied myself to the design of a small ad. On the first day it ran, I received about a dozen phone calls. Then a new problem appeared; responders to my ad were all men, and the first three of them were just looking for sex. I had naively assumed I could save money by starting my new business within my own home, but now there were strangers rather than friends of friends arriving as customers. That ended my widely circulated advertising and conducting business in my home.

I then joined a small group of other therapists in a newly opened spa, which collectively provided advertising, group discounts for our health insurance, and other people nearby for security. Having the support of other people was important and worked well for about a year. Then certain irritating personalities surprisingly unfolded like those in my previous office. One young man constantly complained about how the owner was managing it. Then the gossip and other complaints started increasing, and I no longer looked forward to working there.

Once again, I sought to reestablish control over my surroundings and found a small office to lease by myself. This worked well, at least for maintaining my peaceful surroundings. In the meantime, I had been offered the chance to work two days a week in a physical therapy clinic. Although it didn't pay well, it provided me with valuable experience and additional income.

Within the physical therapy clinic, I was learning and engaged in truly valuable work. However, those were the days when the main principle of physical therapy seemed to be "No pain, no gain." The attitude of the lead physical therapist was that the pain patients experienced was really their fault because "They could have taken themselves to the gym and just worked it out."

When I saw patients after their exercises, it was hard to know whether they were suffering more from their original pain or from their intense exercise regimens. Nevertheless, I did the best I could with people who seemed to appreciate and consistently requested my services. However, I was in way over my head in my understanding of their pain patterns. In addition, I was now on a tight schedule for reading medical notes, placing hot packs, massaging, changing sheets, putting hot packs back in hot water, writing my own notes, and repeating for the next patient. The job was physically and emotionally exhausting.

Once, I learned that the usual massage goal of relieving tense muscles wasn't always appropriate. I did a beautiful job of relieving the tense spinal muscles of one man, but when he got off the table, he couldn't stand up. His tense muscles had been the only thing supporting his unstable spine. Years later I learned that the same principle holds for chiropractic adjustments. Unstable spines can become more unstable with inappropriate adjustments rather than stabilizing and strengthening exercises.

The demand for massage grew, and a second massage therapist was hired, which helped since the other therapist had had somewhat different training and experience so we could confer with each other. We both appreciated the

work and the steady income, but then a hospital adminis-
trator decided it didn't make economic sense to be paying
two people half-time, so they combined the two jobs into
one full-time job. I felt that full time would be beyond my
physical limits and left it to the other younger and stronger
therapist.

I breathed a little easier with improved skills and an
almost-adequate number of private clients. Then I was suddenly confronted with some major economic challenges.
Checks against my bank account unexpectedly started
bouncing, and I was charged large fees. This had happened
because my monthly autopay health insurance of $75 had
suddenly become $300 due to my fiftieth birthday and having
left the group discounted insurance of the spa. (These costs
seem like a bargain in the year 2020, but in the economy of the
early 1990s, they were horrendous.) Then I needed to buy a
wedding gift for one of my sons and had to put it on my credit
card. Then my car engine burned up. Then, as more and more
people were drawn to careers in massage, schools of massage
began offering discount sessions with students.

I had prided myself on being able to live a minimalist
lifestyle so I could do what I loved. I had also strived not to
be associated with what I perceived to be a greedy American
culture. Ironically, in my minimalist lifestyle, I realized I was
becoming more and more obsessed with money. I was seeing
the next patient as part of my rent or car repair bill or groceries, and I spent more than a couple of days a week searching
for quarters in pockets. After five years of this lifestyle, I had
enough. As much as I loved doing massage and was proud of

my minimalist lifestyle, I finally recognized that the need for money was to be respected.

I thought about and began to appreciate the differences between large businesses or government organizations and romantic visions of the independence of small businesses. Small businesses are at the mercy of an inconsistent market-place, which can vary from season to season or with diseases or wars or weather disasters. In contrast, government organizations and large corporations can smooth out the ups and downs of income because they are supported by taxes or capital from both public and private investors.

The small business owner must pay for his or her own sick leave and vacation time either in missed appointments or by hiring someone else. Specialized accounting departments and lawyers minimize their taxes, whereas the small business owner is his or her own accountant with limited knowledge of changing tax laws. Imagine my frustration when I saw that the small profit I made each year was largely swallowed up by the regressive cost of social security, which had previously been partly paid as a benefit by my large hospital employer.

Although I spent some time looking for different jobs, I realized I was most experienced in the institution and department in which I had previously worked. I also didn't want to completely let go of my massage business, so I hoped for a half-time job, which would allow me to continue doing massage in the other halftime. I realized I would be more likely to obtain and handle the demands of such a job in the setting in which I was already familiar.

So back I went to a job with the same department chair, for whom reports were never completed fast enough and back to people complaining and arguing and back to a sitting job. By this time, though, I had learned that there are challenging personalities wherever you go and whatever you do. This knowledge enabled me to manage my reactions on the job while appreciating the steady paycheck, health insurance, paid vacations, and sick leave. Surprising and helpful to me were the coworkers and those from other departments who welcomed me back so warmly and with whom I could now appreciate working as part of a team.

In the meantime, computer technology had advanced from lengthy and tedious programming to point-and-click screens, which greatly increased the efficiency of data analysis and reports. Advances in science concerning cancer were also occurring, and I was just as interested in them as I had always been. Some days I even regretted having to leave that job in the middle of analyzing data so I could hurry to a massage appointment. Then a few years later, the department chairman was replaced by someone who was less of a dictatorial boss, and life in the office became even less stressful.

I continued seeing massage clients in the afternoons and on Saturdays, so I felt I was keeping faith with that second path I had chosen. Years later, when I moved to a small town, I saw that most people were doing at least two jobs. By then it had become normal, even in large cities, since hourly wages were no longer sufficient to cover living expenses for most people.

I managed my split career for another five years until my second husband was dying from cancer and I simply didn't have the time for two jobs. I shed some tears and let go of my independent small massage business, for which I had poured eleven years of my love and energy; unknown to me was that another door was about to open.

Chapter 18

MUSCLE MEMORY

Early in life, memory seemed to just be part of my mind, which was part of my brain, which was in my head. As a child, it seemed that walking was something I did automatically since I had no conscious memory of having learned it. Then I consciously learned to ride a bike, roller-skate, dance, and swim. How wonderful it was to develop to the point of doing those actions automatically because of my muscle memory.

One time, though, I appeared to have lost some of my muscle memory. I had a back injury that limited my usual activities for about a year, and the first time after I had recovered and again mounted a stepladder, I was shaky. Similarly, when I again climbed on my bike, my sense of balance seemed to have disappeared, leaving me shaky and fearful. Fortunately, my muscles rapidly regained their previous memories of balancing.

One of my most surprising examples of muscle memory occurred in my seventieth decade. I was on a cross-county skiing trip in Yellowstone, which was challenging both my balancing and endurance skills. One evening within the lodge, I noticed a wall of shelves containing hundreds of new ice skates in all sizes. *Don't do it, Nancy!* my brain said. *You're in your seventies, and you haven't been ice skating in twenty years. Oh, but I love skating,* I thought as I slowly reached for my size. Almost in a trancelike state, I began putting on and lacing up a pair of skates.

I gingerly stepped out onto the ice and cautiously glided with one leg and then the other and then the other, and immediately I felt so at home. I had that small ice rink all to myself and glided faster and faster in the moonlight, glorying in the feeling and thanking my legs and whole body for its surprising muscular memories.

I have learned that my body isn't limited to the storage of physical skills; it also retains emotions. My first and most vivid experience occurred during my training to be a massage therapist. I had attended a workshop focused on the spinal muscles, in which we attendees took turns massaging and being massaged under the guidance of an experienced instructor. I probably had the tightest back muscles in the group, but after three days of this concentrated massage, my whole body felt wonderfully relaxed. I even felt that I had grown taller.

That night I fell into a deeply relaxed sleep, only to be awakened in the early-morning hours by a frightening nightmare, in which I was screaming, crying, and yelling at my parents. I woke, shaking, and thought about it for most of the next day. *What was that about?* I wondered. The more I thought about it, the more I became convinced that I had never lost the feelings of those years of my youth, in which I had been routinely told, "Don't talk back!" My unexpressed feelings had simply been locked down tightly into the muscles along my spine. Final release had occurred through massage, a dramatic nightmare, and conscious examination the next day.

One form of body-centered therapy, known as Hakomi, furthered my understanding of emotional expressions within the body. These therapists would instruct their clients to listen to statements such as, "I know my mother loves me," and then pay attention to reactions in their bodies, such as a warm feeling or a tightening of the throat.[16]

Most Hakomi therapists had also been trained as psychotherapists, which I hadn't, so I didn't pursue this type of analytical talk with my clients. I did, however, attend a couple of workshops, in which I observed the amazing power of this approach. In one workshop I watched as an instructor skillfully guided the practice client back into childhood through some buried memories.

In another workshop, we students were instructed to massage the thigh of each of our practice clients and then to pay close attention to any reactions they expressed. My practice client said that "it felt good," but she also said that while I was massaging her thigh, she felt something near her left ankle. As instructed, I then asked her to describe exactly what she had felt—what color it was, what shape, and what size.

She said it was gray and about the size of a nickel.

We were instructed not to offer any reactions other than "Oh?" or "Hmmm."

Suddenly she said, "My sister's brace!" She then shared the memory that had been awakened in her leg. She had learned to walk by watching her older sister, who walked with a brace. Her left leg had bothered her most of her life despite different types of therapies. This was the first time she had made the connection and was feeling relief just from knowing the origin of her leg troubles.

I also learned how sensory information could be absorbed by my own hands. In my eleven years as a massage therapist, my hands became more and more sensitive to the muscles and bones in other people's bodies. Year by year, my hands learned as they felt muscle fibers that were tight, ropey, knotted, or slippery. Sometimes I encountered hot areas and could feel heat rising through my hands and entire body.

I learned that I could release tight spots by applying pressure that wasn't too much and not too little. Sometimes the person being massaged had memories awakened or felt sensations in other parts of his or her body. Although I no longer practice massage, I still receive massage, pay careful attention to dreams, and try to be sensitive to thoughts arising not only in my mind but also to feelings that arise throughout my entire body.

Chapter 19

EXPANDING HEALTH RESEARCH

Three grief-filled months after the death of both my husband and my massage business, an amazing new job opportunity unexpectedly appeared. Ever since I had begun working in cancer statistics, I had cringed at the thought of the brutal treatments usually required to remove, stop, or at least slow the spread of cancer. Chemotherapy, radiation, and surgery were unofficially referred to as "poison," "burn," and "cut." Some side effects could be lessened but rarely removed, and most simply had to be endured.

During the decades when I was analyzing the results of these conventional treatments, I was also going to health food stores, where I was buying a variety of herbs, supplements, and books. I was continually seeking different ideas concerning my own and other people's health. Many books promoted alternative ways of treating cancer and provided dramatic testimonials. I had had enough training in research methods to know individual anecdotes wouldn't be sufficient evidence for recommendations of these treatments; however, some stories were compelling.

When all three conventional treatments of my husband's sarcoma failed to control its painful local and metastatic spread, we felt we had nothing to lose. I returned to the health food stores, and, using recently developed computer search tools, I found newly published books and other reports. I settled on one combination herbal treatment that seemed reasonable and had many stories of success. I would read those stories at the request of my husband when he began taking this herbal tonic.

Sadly, this highly promoted herbal formula didn't stop or slow down his rapidly spreading cancer, and he died about two months later. But what if he had used it earlier? What if there had been more reliable research about when and how to use it? What if there had been other natural substances that could have complemented or lessened the side effects of his conventional treatments?

One day a few months after my husband died, I learned about a timely opportunity from a contact in another department. A researcher at the School of Public Health and a surgeon at the Cancer Center had received a grant from the newly established Office for Alternative Medicine within the National Institutes of Health (NIH). That grant was to fund a center to review the evidence of safety and efficacy for herbal and other alternative treatments for cancer. I knew I would be a perfect fit for the job based on my years of experience in both conventional cancer research and the many alternative approaches being promoted within health food stores and the massage community. Big lesson—it pays to have colleagues in other departments who know about your qualifications and passions. You never know when they might pass along key information at just the right time.

I landed that half-time job in a building just a short walk from my current job. I immediately plunged into reading the background stories of eighteen proposed alternative treatments for cancer. The first step was to learn what research had already been published. This wasn't as easy as it would be today, since almost none of the medical journals were posted on the Internet in 1995. Obtaining the actual printed copies of those journals required numerous walks to the Library of the Medical Center, hauling stacks of heavy, hard-bound journal volumes to a copy machine, and then returning to my office with copies to be indexed, filed, and read.

One of the first treatments I reviewed was the herbal formula my husband had tried. To my chagrin, the testimonies with which I had been so previously impressed fell apart on subsequent examination. Of the dozen testimonials, some were by people who had only recently been diagnosed, some were by people who hadn't actually had cancer, and some hadn't reported enough information to draw any conclusions. Even with all my training in research methods, I had overlooked these deficiencies because I had been so anxious to find a cure for my husband. Big lesson! Everyone is at risk of being led astray by personal biases. This is why blinded clinical trials are so essential.

In further reviews, I uncovered fascinating stories of how conventional scientists and others had developed theories, tested those theories, and formed conclusions that were either justified or not. Many such efforts had begun in good faith, but their research had been limited to animals, their clinical studies had failed to recruit enough patients, or they hadn't been able to follow participants long enough to observe meaningful differences in outcomes. Typically, clinical trial participants had either received or were currently receiving conventional therapies, which made it difficult to disentangle the effects of conventional versus alternative treatments. Examples were reviewed on the website for the center and in a published article.[17]

Reviewing clinical trials wasn't a problem since I had had a lot of experience in that field. However, I had had minimal experience with laboratory research, and many new concepts and terms had been introduced into the field of tumor biology in the decades since I had been in graduate school. By the following year, I realized I was way out on a limb as far as knowing what I was doing. There were knowledgeable faculty available, but most were receiving little or no compensation from our grant, and their time was limited. It had also become apparent to me that any knowledge about cancer research I had gained on the job wasn't being acknowledged by those who had doctorates, even if their doctorates had not been focused on cancer research. I knew I would either need to let go of the job I loved or go back to school to catch up on advances in both laboratory and clinical research.

The thought of returning to school for more years of study was terrifying. However, it was also intriguing, and the hospital would pay my tuition, so I couldn't pass up on such an opportunity. In my first class back in school, an expert geneticist led us skillfully through an introduction to current knowledge concerning genetics and cancer. I felt my heart beating faster with excitement and knew I had made the right decision.

The next years were so full of working and learning that I had no time to sink further into grieving. Although there was constant stress in that job, there were also excitement and fun. I even had a chance to combine my previous massage career with current research efforts when I coauthored an article concerning massage for patients with cancer.[18] What kept me going were receiving monthly massages, commuting by bike, swimming, and doing step aerobics at the YMCA.

Research for my doctoral dissertation gave me a further chance to explore questions concerning nutrition and cancer. I had read and heard that patients who were newly diagnosed with cancer typically changed their eating habits, but little research had shown if or to what extent this was happening. Knowing how challenging it was to change habits, I designed a study to explore the question and find out whether any changes appeared to be in healthy directions.

I conducted my study among patients in one of the clinics at the cancer center. My questionnaire asked the participants whether they had changed their diets and, if so, whether they were now eating more, less, or about the same amounts of whole grains, fruits, vegetables, and meats. We learned that most patients had been overweight or obese before and after their initial treatments and that 40 percent of them were eating less than the currently recommended five-a-day amounts of fruits and vegetables. This was true even among those who said they were now eating more fruits and vegetables.[19] We also learned that most were consuming either inadequate or excessive amounts of five key nutrients: folate, vitamin A, iron, selenium, and calcium.[20]

The following year, I received my doctorate in public health (DrPH); and just a few short years later, I retired.

Chapter 20

WORK, PLAY, AND HEALTH IN RETIREMENT

On my first day of retirement, I flew to Colorado to enjoy one of my rarely indulged in passions—cross-country skiing. I wasn't that good at it, but I was getting better. I loved snow—an odd thing for someone who had landed in Texas. Understandably, flying north to play in the snow for a week is a lot different from living in a long, dark, and cold winter for months at a time. If I had lived in a place with long winters, I might have learned to do downhill skiing, but the one time I had tried it, I spent too much time freezing while waiting for or riding on the ski lift and then experiencing just a few minutes of terror as I too rapidly descended the mountain.

Cross-country skiing, in contrast, consisted of constant physical movement over less dramatic terrain. I loved the feeling of gliding over the snow and even taking turns with others to make new trails, which required slower and more effort-filled stepping. Cross-country skis have scales on the bottoms to grip the snow so you can ski uphill as well as down. Constant effort is required as you glide, climb, or sidestep your way up, down, and around hills. Rewards of all this effort are a great workout and, with the proper clothing, always feeling warm. Even at temperatures around zero degrees, I often needed to unzip my jacket or remove a sweater to keep from sweating too much.

Following my brief winter vacation, I turned my attention to preparing my home for sale by cleaning out the garage, remodeling the kitchen, and having the roof replaced, which took about two years. This activity was interspersed with a month in Costa Rica, a week hiking the Inca Trail in Peru, and camping in the mountains of New Mexico.

Finally, I had my home in the condition for which I had been striving for the fifteen years in which I had lived there. I had removed carpet, refinished the wood floors, replaced the old insulation in the attic, had the walls insulated, had central air conditioning installed, replaced the single-pane windows with double-paned ones, painted the house inside and out, torn out two walls, and added two skylights.

My home was comfortable and beautiful; nevertheless, it wasn't easy to sell. Not only was the year 2010, at the bottom of the sellers' market, but my home had three bedrooms with only one bathroom. No one seemed to have any interest in a home with only one bathroom. No matter how a few architects and I analyzed the floor plan and structure, there was simply no way to add another bathroom. Not only did the house lack a second bath, but it was located next to a busy railroad track.

My house sat on the market for half a year, mostly unseen. Then suddenly there was a buyer, who had seen it while driving past on his way to the foreclosed house down the street. He was a bachelor who had no concern about having only one bathroom, and the railroad reminded him of his childhood home. Within the next month, I had sold my house and moved to the small town of Wimberley in central Texas.

Although the market value of homes in Houston had fallen, it had also fallen in Wimberley. I downsized to a townhouse and had money left over for remodeling. Part of me didn't look forward to the thought of once again remodeling a home, but this time I had enough money to hire professional help so it wouldn't take a decade to accomplish. In a couple of months, I was able to move in and settle into a new life.

Due to my monthly pension from the Texas Teachers' Retirement Fund and social security payments, I didn't need to work and was able to follow interesting volunteer opportunities. I remained more active in research than I could have predicted. As research co- chair for the Mastocytosis Society (now the Mast Cell Society), a patient advocacy organization for a rare immune system disorder, others and I conducted a survey and published two articles concerning patient experiences.[21,22]

Although this new research was interesting and much appreciated by the society members, it was also challenging, and I no longer had access to the expensive analytical software paid for by my previous hospital employer. Once again,

I found myself buried in thousands of data cells within Excel files. Continually we, the two lead coauthors, e-mailed back and forth and talked for hours over shared computer screens. We were constantly checking and cleaning up the data before daring to do any analysis or accept any results.

In working with a chiropractor, I gained valuable insights into the painful conditions of spinal misalignments and fibromyalgia.[23] This too involved many hours of counting, writing, and revising. The hours of time and energy I spent in both projects were rewarded, not in money but in knowledge gained and opportunities to work with wonderful people, who cared about using the best scientific methods possible with limited funding to help people with serious health challenges.

Another unexpected volunteer passion happened after I discovered the artesian spring north of Wimberley, known as "Jacob's Well." I was fascinated with its clear waters rising from deep within the earth, which led me to meet others with the same fascination. Together we learned and shared knowledge about the relationship of water to the surrounding plants, animals, and land. Then I became a member of the county master naturalist program and a volunteer tour guide at the spring. Here I was in a new town with my brain striving to learn not only the names of new people but also new plants and animals. I remembered that once upon a time, I had dreamed of being a nature guide, and it was now happening in my seventies.

I continued traveling north most winters for cross-country skiing in wonderful places such as Oregon, Yellowstone, Glacier

National Park, and Alaska. Finally, at the age of seventy-nine, however, I had trouble keeping up with younger members of the Sierra Club groups, so I had to drop out only to ski with one or two others at a slower pace.

I believe I was the healthiest and probably did my best skiing during the Yellowstone trip in 2012. How ironic that a week later, I had a mammogram that detected a suspicious lump in my breast, which turned out to be malignant. Of course, it was terrifying. I didn't however, think, *Why me?* I had spent too many years analyzing breast cancer occurrence and survival rates to have any illusions. I knew how common breast cancer was, especially after menopause.

Like many women, I had been paranoid about my breasts for decades and I dreaded the annual mammograms. I had even looked at my sagging breasts in the mirror and thought, *these breasts are no longer either useful or pleasant to look at. Why don't they just regress? What would it take to cut them off?*

I decided to have a mastectomy rather than a lumpectomy since I didn't see that there was that much left to save anyway. Although the other breast wasn't known to have any cancer in it, I didn't see any point in keeping one sagging breast, about which I would be constantly worried. I also decided to have only one axillary lymph node removed on each side. If that one turned out to be malignant, my biggest worry, I would then decide what to do. Fortunately, no malignancy was found in those axillary nodes, and I breathed a huge sigh of relief.

Because my tumor was found to be estrogen-receptor positive, this meant that taking a tiny anti-estrogen pill once a day for five years should prevent any remaining malignant cells from growing. It wasn't that simple, though, because lack of estrogen also interfered with bone metabolism, which required other pills; however, the combined treatment managed to keep me free of cancer and just on the border of osteoporosis. All those decades of breast cancer research by thousands of people since the 1970s were now benefitting me and many other women. If I had been diagnosed in the 1970s, my only options would have been chemotherapy and radiation. I took those anti-hormone and other pills for five years, and as far as anyone knows, I remain cancer free nine years later.

That first month after the mastectomy was challenging but manageable. A nerve block had been done at the time of the surgery, so I never felt what I would call true pain. In addition, my years of massaging and being massaged had provided me with an exquisite ability to locate and analyze pain and other sensations in my body. What I felt as the incision and nerves were healing was more like something between an itch and a tickle. I also felt phantom breasts, but they weren't painful, and I kind of liked their memory. I'm grateful that I never felt a need to take any of the OxyContin opioid pills sent home with me.

I could have spent the following months grieving for my lost breasts and terrified about the risk of impending death, but I didn't for a couple of reasons. First, I was anxious to get back to my life in Wimberley, where the annual butterfly event was about to take place. Second, I had previously signed up with the Sierra Club for a trip to Ireland the following month, and I saw no reason to cancel it.

I've heard it said that people who receive a diagnosis of cancer develop a new appreciation for life. Not me! I was doing fine and already had a deep appreciation of life without the interruption of any kind of disease. Furthermore, I'm not impressed with the concept of lessons being taught through disease. One of the saddest things I have ever heard was from a friend who was managing to live a full life despite having multiple sclerosis. When she received a subsequent diagnosis of leukemia, she had begged God not to teach her another lesson with disease.

My trip to Ireland was combined with a side trip to Sweden to scatter the ashes of my lover, who had died twenty-three years before. It was another of many trips of a lifetime. I had no time to dwell on missing breasts, healing incisions, or risk of death. I am still traveling and enjoying life in my eighties, and I'm especially enjoying the freedom of movement without a bra.

Part Six

BASIC SKILLS

Chapter 21

MAGICIAN IN THE GROCERY STORE

One day while I was standing in the produce department of my local supermarket, a young man walked up and said, "Excuse me, ma'am."

Uh-oh, I thought. *He's going to ask for money.*

However, he simply held up two large cans of baby milk formula and said, "I'm trying to decide which kind of baby formula I should buy for my son. Should I buy this one with iron or this other one without iron?"

"Well," I said, "what kind does your wife usually buy?"

"Oh, my wife left, and she's doing whatever she's doing, and I'm just trying to raise my son by myself. He was born premature, but he's doing better; I just want to help him grow and be strong."

"Aw," I said. "That's tough. What does his doctor or nurse say?"

"Oh, that clinic is on the other side of town; it's too far and too hard to get an appointment."

"Well," I said, "iron can cause digestive problems, so I wouldn't buy any with iron unless a doctor suggests it. Is your son eating any solid foods yet?"

"No, he's just drinking milk."

"Really?" I said. "How old is he?"

"He's a year old."

"Oh," I said, "he should be eating some solid foods by now. You could give him some plain cooked cereal, and if he handles that, you could then give him some cereal with iron. Again, though, I wouldn't do that unless a doctor or nurse suggests it."

"Oh," he said, "that's a good idea. Thank you so much; you've really been helpful."

His cell phone rang, and he turned and left. I continued my shopping, pleased that I had been able to use my knowledge of public health and experience as a mother to help someone.

He must have been a magician, though, because when I opened my purse at the checkout stand, my wallet had disappeared. In the next forty-five minutes, he and his accomplice, who had apparently done the actual lifting of the wallet, spent $500 on new tires, a battery, assorted items from Target, and even coffee from Starbucks.

Learning how to avoid being conned is an important basic skill. Lesson number one is to slow down, pay attention, and not swallow everything from a stranger before sharing your brilliant knowledge.

Lesson number two. Be more suspicious when someone says something that doesn't make sense, such as a story about a one-year-old child who isn't eating solid food.

Lesson number three. Keep the contact information for your bank and credit card company in your cell phone or at least separate from your wallet to avoid wasting valuable time searching for them when reporting the theft or loss.

Chapter 22

ELEMENTARY CARPENTRY

One of my most memorable times in my progressive elementary school had been the two years in which both boys and girls had a class in woodworking. In this class, we were taught important skills with simple tools. For example, how not to hit your thumb when using a hammer, measuring wood, cutting it, counting to ten every so often so that your saw blade could cool down, wetting wood so that the grain would rise before its initial sanding. Developing those skills produced a birdhouse and later several shelves in different homes. One time, however, I began what I thought would be a simple project, but it was surprisingly complex.

We needed a shed to replace the garage my husband and I (mainly my husband) had just remodeled into a bedroom. *This should be simple*, I thought.

I drew up plans on graph paper based on four-foot-by-eight-foot sheets of plywood. By making the walls and floor the same size as the plywood, I expected that I could cleverly avoid unnecessary sawing. I then bought the plywood, the support lumber, and the nails. I began assembling the pieces in our backyard by first laying the lumber down in a rectangle with the boards on their wide sides. First mistake! The nails weren't long enough to go all the way through to the next pieces at the corners. Not realizing this initial mistake, I returned to the store for longer nails, but the only ones long enough were so thick that I knew they would split the wood.

After returning home and staring at the lumber for a while, it finally dawned on me that if I turned the lumber over so the narrow side was on the ground, the original nails would work. I must say that I felt incredibly embarrassed by my stupidity and was glad no one had witnessed it. Finally, I assembled a rectangular box of lumber and plywood with an open top.

Then I considered the roof, which would be slanted to allow for water to run off and made of fiberglass to let in the light. But how large a piece of fiberglass should I buy? A flat roof would have been easy—just a little larger than the dimensions of the shed. But how large did a slanted roof need to be?

Suddenly, something connected in my brain—a slanted roof would be the hypotenuse of a triangle. Although I had mostly struggled with basic arithmetic and mathematics in school, I had always enjoyed geometry, because I could see its relationships in diagrams. Visions of angles and formulas began swimming in my mind—hypotenuse, $a^2 + b^2 = c^2$, side, angle, side, and so forth. I couldn't remember which formula would answer my question, but I knew I could find the key in an old geometry textbook I had inexplicably saved.

There it was: the hypotenuse (fiberglass roof) would be the longest side, and it would be equal to the square root of the sum of the lengths squared of the other two sides. Wow! All those geometric puzzles, and finally I had a chance to apply that knowledge. I solved the equation, bought the appropriately sized panels of fiberglass, and finished the construction of the shed. It fulfilled its purpose and lasted for some years until the house was sold. All students studying geometry should have the chance to build something.

Chapter 23

TRADING CARS WITH CHINA AND OTHER ECONOMIC LESSONS

My car was fifteen years old and had been driven about one hundred and fifty thousand miles. With the guidance and help of a true friend, we had rebuilt the engine. Then the AC quit working, and then the steering column cracked, and I had to spend the better part of a week looking into auto salvage yards for a replacement. These repair issues occurred in addition to the usual brake, spark plug, and other routine maintenance.

Although I was proud of what I had learned in the process, I realized car repair was becoming a second career, in which I wasn't that interested. I had some savings, but no matter how much I added to them, the price of cars always increased just beyond reach.

Then one day I saw an ad that said, "Bicycle in China—$3,000." It was just the amount of money in my bank account. But what about the car? *Well*, I thought, *I've always wanted to see China for myself, and if not now, when? Besides, I'd rather arrive in my old age with a good strong set of legs and some stories than a car anyway.*

I sent the money, and by the following July of 1982, I was bicycling in China. This was just a few years following the recognition of China by the United States after the long Cold War ban on travel between the two countries. Our group of American cyclists was only the second one to have a bicycle tour.

We visited Beijing, the Great Wall, Nanjing, Wuxi, and Shanghai. We cycled on country roads and traveled by boat on the Grand Canal. Oh, the things we saw, the people we met, and the foods we ate! I learned how truly ancient the Chinese culture was as we learned that the sidewalks that we walked on and the carvings and tiles that we saw had been created thousands of years ago. I learned how physically strong the Chinese people were as I witnessed them carrying enormous loads on their bicycles. I learned about overpopulation up close and personal as we cycled on streets or walked on sidewalks overflowing with people.

At that time, the Chinese government was teaching English on TV. Often one of the thousands of cyclists around us would approach to satisfy their curiosity with newly learned English phrases. "Hello, are you from America?" "How old are you?" "What is your job?" "Do you have children?"

One day, the brake fell off my rented bike, causing me to

tumble over the handlebars and onto the street. The surrounding crowd of cyclists picked me up, checked to see whether I was okay, and repaired my bike. We were on our way.

The trip ended in three weeks, but the Chinese people I saw in the subsequent news were no longer anonymous figures on a TV screen. They were people for whom I now felt new respect and a personal connection.

The following year (still driving my old car), my youngest son called to let me know he had just seen a boat and trailer for $500 at a garage sale. I bought the boat and trailer, and we both worked to repair its damaged mast and hull. All the work was worth it when we finally sailed.

At the end of a second weekend of sailing, we loaded it onto my trailer and cautiously pulled out into the intersection when the light turned green. Suddenly, my son yelled, "Watch out!" as someone ran his red light and crashed into the boat and trailer.

I watched it all happen in slow motion in the rearview mirror as the boat and trailer rolled sideways across the intersection. Miraculously, no one was hurt. The man who had run the light stopped his car, came running over, and admitted his responsibility. Another man came over to us as a witness and offered to help by towing the boat and trailer to his nearby yard. The next day, an insurance company called and asked me how much money I wanted.

"Enough to replace the boat and trailer," I said.

Two days later I had a check for $2,000 in my hands. Two days after that, I met a casual friend who was selling her car. *Hmmm, that's just the kind of car I have been wanting, and she* *is asking for $2,000.* I felt like I was acting in a play and just had to speak the right lines. I bought her car and sold my old car for $200 to a mechanic. So that is how $3,000 saved for a car was traded for an unforgettable trip in China and how $500 spent on a boat became a $2,000 car.

Decades after my car, China, and boat adventures were history, I was again driving a fifteen-year-old car with over a hundred thousand miles on it. That car was bigger, as were the repairs—$1,100 to replace the AC, $400 for brakes, and $1,500 for a rebuilt transmission. Seven months after that, the rebuilt transmission with a six-month warrantee jammed. I let it sit for a few months while I took the bike or bus to work and then reluctantly spent another $1,500 to have the transmission rebuilt.

Ah, I thought, *now everything is working so I'll sell the car before anything else happens.* Life sometimes happens quickly, though. The following morning, while enjoying a leisurely Sunday breakfast, I suddenly heard a loud crash. I ran out of the house just in time to see a large SUV pulling away from the smashed front end of my car. As the other car was also damaged and moving slowly, I had plenty of time to write down its license plate number and call the police, who arrived in about ten minutes. Finding the other car was easy, since the police simply followed its tire tracks down the street, around the corner, and up into a garage.

Surprisingly, the story of that collision didn't involve drugs or alcohol. A young man had been driving home while eating a hamburger, which he dropped on the floor and bent down to retrieve. He had panicked after the collision, afraid that his last month on parole would be revoked. When the police introduced us to each other, the first words out of his mouth were, "My aunt has a lot of money; my mother and aunt will take care of everything."

He didn't know that I was fresh out of support groups, where I was learning how to disentangle myself from the troubles of others. "You leave your mother out of this!" I yelled. "Otherwise, you will never grow up!"

While the police officer filled out a report and radioed his headquarters, we then proceeded to have our own unexpected-encounter session seated in the shade of a tree on that hot August day. We must have talked for an hour about prison, jobs, his volunteer work, alcoholism, and drugs.

I had already called my insurance company and found to my relief that I had spent the extra money for insurance against uninsured motorists. I received compensation for the appraised value of the car, plus the cost of two transmissions and the other major repairs of the past year. Keeping all those annoying paper receipts had been worth it. The insurance company even negotiated a payback system so the other driver eventually repaid my deductible.

Fair as that compensation was, however, it wasn't enough to replace my car with one of younger age or lower mileage, and the thought of searching for such a used car made me tired. I then imagined myself buying a new car on credit and facing years of stress while trying to keep up with payments, repairs, and other expenses.

Rather than immediately facing such a stressful financial future, I decided to at least delay it. I wouldn't buy another car immediately; I would just see how long I could function by relying solely on my bike and the Houston bus system. Suddenly, I felt physically lighter.

I then used the $3,000 insurance payment to pay off many months on my home mortgage. After just a few months of not having to buy car insurance, tags, inspections, and repairs, I had surplus money in my checking account. I then opened my first adult savings account and watched it grow. Three years later, I was able to pay off my home mortgage and then added the money no longer needed for those payments into my savings account. I functioned for five and a half years without a car.

Although I was inconvenienced during my years without a car, it wasn't as much as one might have expected. I discovered that bus service was more regular than I was, which encouraged me to have more discipline in my morning routine. Whenever I waited for the bus, I listened to the news or Spanish lessons on my cassette player. After six months limited to biking to the store or walking to the bus stop, I lost ten pounds either from the increase in physical activity or from not buying cans of carbonated fruit drinks because they added too much weight to my bike.

I began to enjoy the challenge of solving transportation puzzles for new areas of town with different bus routes. Two to three times a year, I drove out of town in rental cars, which were fun to pick up—all clean and ready to go. For the first time, I was able to pay for airline tickets without depending on my credit card, and I took some wonderful trips, which were a fair trade for letting go of my car. After five and a half years of this lifestyle, I was also five years beyond the age of my eligibility for social security, so I received a lump-sum payment, which then enabled me to buy a brand-new car and begin a debt-free life in retirement.

Chapter 24

MEASURING THE EARTH WITH A STICK

You can learn a lot by browsing a friend's bookshelf. Two decades after rediscovering the basic principles of geometry so I could put a roof on a shed, I stumbled on another instance of "applied geometry" within the book *Cosmos* by Carl Sagan.[24] It filled in a gap in my elementary school understanding about why Christopher Columbus had begun his famous voyage in 1492. This chapter is my attempt to summarize what I learned from Carl Sagan's book.

In the third century before our common era (BCE), a man by the name of Eratosthenes lived in Alexandria, Egypt. He was director of the world's greatest library, a poet, philosopher, mathematician, and generally curious person. One day he read that in a remote Egyptian outpost at noon on the longest day of the year, a stick stuck in the ground cast no shadow. (People knew it was noon because the sun was directly overhead as indicated by its reflection in the water at the bottom of a deep well.)

He wondered whether that lack of shadow would also be true in his city of Alexandria. To find out, he stuck a stick of the same length in the ground at the same time and watched. Strangely, the stick in his city did cast a shadow. *Why would that be?* he wondered.

He reasoned that if the earth was flat, as everyone perceived it to be, and the rays of the sun were essentially parallel because the sun was so far away, then equal lengths of sticks in both cities at the same time should have cast either no shadows or shadows of the same length. Because one city did have shadows and the other didn't, he reasoned that the earth must be curved.

The Earth at Noon on the Summer Solstice
Flat or Curved?

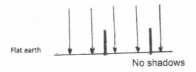

Flat earth
No shadows

Curved earth
Shadow

*Adapted from diagram on page 15 of Cosmos[24]

This information would have been monumental enough in any century, but Eratosthenes didn't stop there. He then assumed a right angle (90 degrees), where an imaginary parallel ray of the sun would project toward the center of the earth in the city with no shadow. He then measured the length of the shadow of the stick in Alexandria and projected an imaginary line from the end of the shadow to the top of the same stick and measured the angle formed, which he found to be 7 degrees. Next, he used a previously accepted geometric principle—*If two parallel lines are crossed by a third line, the alternate interior angles are equal*—to show that the angle of 7 degrees between the end of the shadow and the imaginary line to the sun's ray would be the same as the angle at the center of the earth.

Finally, he hired someone to pace the distance between the two cities and learned that it was about eight hundred kilometers (fifty miles in US customary units). Since 7 degrees is about one-fiftieth of a full circle of 360 degrees, the distance between Alexandria and the other city must have been about one-fiftieth of the circumference of the earth. Using simple arithmetic, he showed that eight hundred kilometers times fifty would indicate a total earth circumference of forty thousand kilometers (twenty-five thousand miles). Amazingly, this estimate determined three centuries BCE is within just a few miles of the current estimate.

Finding the Circumference of the Earth

based on parallel rays of the sun

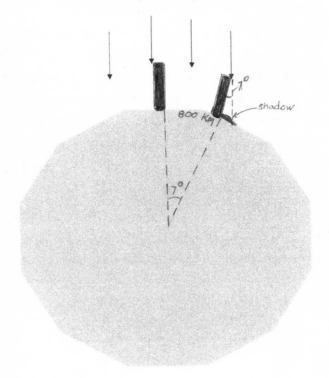

Divide 360 degrees of the earth's full circle by 7 degrees = 51.4 sections

Multiply 51.4 times 800 kilometers per section = 41,120 kilometers

(Or 51.4 X 500 miles = 25,000 miles)*

*Adapted from diagram on page 15 of Cosmos[24]

Knowledge of the shape and size of the earth spread and was preserved among Arabic scholars, who spread it as far as China. Speculation grew about the possibilities of sailing around the earth, and there were many attempts. However, such voyages didn't have adequate methods for preserving food for such a long journey and lacked accurate methods for estimating longitude. Columbus, who was aware of the estimated distance, was able to convince the king and queen of Spain to finance his voyage because he used the shortest estimate possible and cheated on his calculations. If his ship hadn't bumped into the American continent, it would have simply been another ship lost at sea.

So it was that the curiosity of a librarian about a difference in shadows and his use of logical thinking rather than magic or divine revelation revealed both the shape and size of the earth almost eighteen hundred years before anyone was able to navigate it.

Chapter 25

LEARNING THE SUBJUNCTIVE

What the heck is the subjunctive? I wondered. I had heard about it in connection with the verb endings in Spanish and French, and it seemed to be a source of annoyance to many people. I was glad that I hadn't had to worry about it in English … or so I thought. Then I began to learn about it in adult evening Spanish classes and became intrigued with its implications.

Subjunctive endings of verbs are used when one is talking about a state of being that doesn't actually exist or about which one has no control. Examples would include one person wanting someone else to do something (I wish he would call me) or wishing that something had happened in the past that hadn't happened (If I had studied harder, I would have passed the test). Even events at some unknown time in the future would qualify as unreal; that is, subjunctive (When she comes, we will leave).

We usually indicate these situations in English by using the word *would*, which isn't apparent to us because we are so used to saying it. When we learn a new language, however, we must consciously become aware of differences in how words and word endings are used. Newly learned subjunctive endings of verbs bring these unreal or uncontrollable situations to our conscious attention.

Could it be that acknowledging limited control over other people or situations is something we have lost in societies of native English speakers? Does this loss often lead us into a false sense of the power of our own influence over the actions of others? Of course, it is possible to influence others, but this is different from *controlling* them.

After becoming more aware of the subjunctive tenses, I began to observe that expectations of control often appeared to be associated with arrogance and frustration. Is it realistic, for example, for a parent to expect his or her child to have the career he or she either had or wanted? Is it realistic for one nation to collectively think it can control the actions of another nation?

Promoting a certain type of government to another nation while still struggling to define and manage its own type of government would seem to be doomed to failure and frustration. On the other hand, cultivating skills of influence, which acknowledge limitations and encourage change by example, would seem to have a better chance of success. If a nation or society focused on the betterment of its own type of government, any apparent advantages might then influence other nations. At least, such conduct might decrease frustrations and even war-like actions.

Chapter 26

REMEDIAL SINGING

"I love to sing, loud and long and clear!" says the song sung by the movie character Mary Poppins. And I did love to sing, trying to mimic the high, clear voices of popular song artists of the 1940s and '50s. "Please stop singing," said my mother. "You're flat, and it's giving me a headache."

What was "flat"? Why didn't I ask? I might have learned that it simply meant being lower than the appropriate note or notes. But I didn't ask, so I didn't learn, and I simply stopped singing, especially at home.

Neither of my parents sang or played a musical instrument or even listened to music. Strangely, my father seemed very anxious for me to learn to play the drum and signed me up for drum lessons when I went to elementary school. I, on the other hand, was fascinated by the trombone—not especially by its sound but by its long U-shaped tube, which slid back and forth.

Nevertheless, I began drum lessons—not on a drum but on a rubber "practice pad" as my parents requested. I'm sure it saved their hearing and peace of mind, but the lack of sound had no reward for me. Practicing time diminished to almost nothing and was soon abandoned.

A few years later, my young brother entered elementary school and was also encouraged to join the school band. This time my father wasn't around to urge the drum on him, but I was there to talk him into playing the trombone. This he did, although I don't know why. It was a poor fit for him since a special wire handle had to be added so he could extend the slide. It must have been awkward, and he soon gave it up. What a waste of effort it is to wish for someone else to do what one wanted and failed to do.

In the third grade, a music class emphasizing singing was added to our other subjects. My eager anticipation, however, was quickly replaced with terror in our first class. The teacher directed each student to come to the front of the room and sing alone and without any piano accompaniment in front of all the other students. My throat immediately tightened, and I barely squeaked out a few words. I felt my face turn hot and red.

We were then assigned seats in the order of how well we had sung. The best singers were placed in the back rows and the worst singers in the front rows, along with those known as "behavior problems." I landed in the second row only because I wasn't a "behavior problem." Despite my public humiliation as a terrible singer, I sang because I just couldn't resist the music. I simply tried to blend my voice with the other voices, hoping no one would hear my deficiency.

Did I have a *bad* voice? Who knows? Nobody gave us any instructions on breathing or using abdominal muscles or on exhaling or opening our mouths to shape words. Many children seemed to sing or listen to music at home, but I didn't. Was I "tone deaf"? All the children in our school received a hearing test, and I recall there being some discussion about my left ear. However, nothing was done about it. As an adult, I have had a few hearing tests that noted some loss in the high-frequency range but not enough (yet) to warrant hearing aids.

All the way through my teen years, I continued to sing in school and church and whenever there was any group singing at a football game, at a party, or on a bus. After college, though, there didn't seem to be much opportunity to sing along with others. Sadly, I was afraid to sing to my babies. For decades, though, I sang to popular songs on the radio or records but only if no one else was around. If others were around, I sang silently in my mind.

During college, I became a confirmed atheist and for decades enjoyed the freedom of spending Sunday mornings outside rather than in a church. One year, however, I suddenly realized I missed the singing. Then I occasionally started going to the only church that had rewritten hymn lyrics so they were no longer limited to praising a male God, the Unitarian-Universalist Church. The music and lyrics were so beautiful that I cried as I again sought to blend my voice with those around me.

"Too soon, old; too late smart." I have often had to acknowledge the truth of this expression variously attributed to Dutch, German, Scandinavian, and other sources. In my mid-fifties, while grieving the death of my second husband, I had a new thought about singing. *I'll bet that if I paid money to a voice teacher, they could help me to at least improve my singing voice.*

What a difference it makes when you acknowledge a deficiency and ask for help from someone who wants to teach and share what he or she loves. My first voice teacher taught me that mimicking a note really was possible next to someone with a better ear who could coach me to sing higher or lower. I learned to shape my mouth and became conscious of my muscular soft palate, which could change its shape. As with any set of muscles, it became stronger with practice. I also learned that ordinary conversational speech uses about five notes, while singing uses a wider range of notes. Not singing for decades had diminished my ability to reach notes in that wider range.

In my middle 70s, I joined a wonderful community chorus, which fortunately didn't require auditions. Still feeling like an imposter, I sought the help of the director, who agreed to take me on as a student. I learned from this calm and knowledgeable teacher that my voice was breaking and routinely missing notes largely because I was running out of air. Focusing on abdominal muscles and finally turning off my straining throat muscles began to help. Weekly rehearsals with a variety of knowledgeable and cheerful directors provided the practice I needed.

Although I sang with that group for several years, I continued to feel paranoid about my voice. Then one day someone told me she had joined the chorus because she had heard my clear, high voice. I almost fainted. Sometimes one needs to unlearn what he or she has learned in his or her family and school so he or she can clear the way for real learning.

Part Seven

LESSONS IN NATURE

Chapter 27

LOST IN THE WOODS

One of my most memorable days in elementary school was when our teacher asked us all to stand and face the windows. Then she said, "You are now facing east, which is the direction from which the sun rises. North is on your left, and south is on your right. Now turn in the opposite direction; that is west, where the sun sets."

I was so excited. I thought, *Now I can always know where I am.* Although I realized it would be a challenge with rain or darkness, I had also learned about magnetic north, which could be found with a compass. I began to read lots of books about exploring and additional ways of finding direction. Secretly, I kind of wished I would sometime get lost and then be smart enough to find my way. A couple of decades later, my wish was granted.

We didn't really mean to go deep into the woods; we had

no food, extra clothing, matches, water, or a compass. We were only taking a walk around a campground by a lake. It was Labor Day weekend, and people were setting off firecrackers by the lake, so we assumed we had plenty of noise to mark the location.

My husband was walking with our three-year-old son, and I was carrying our one-year-old son on my back. I was walking slowly to look at the plants, while my husband was moving rapidly to get a good workout. We were walking on what my husband said was an "old logging road," which was something I had never heard of, although it seemed reasonable. Eventually, the road dwindled to a path and then to nothing.

Neither of us had had any experience walking in the woods, but I had read many stories about people getting lost in woods, so I asked that we slow down, but this was ignored. Eventually, lengthening shadows indicated to both of us that we needed to get back to our campground.

"It's this way," he said.

"No, it's that way," I said.

"But the sound is coming from over there," he said.

"No, I hear it coming from over there," I said.

Woods Lesson #1: Sounds can be confusing in thick woods since they can be both absorbed and echoed, appearing to bounce around from different directions.

After several failed attempts to locate the logging road, we had to reluctantly admit that we were lost. We tried to recall the various advice we had read or heard about finding directions when lost, especially on a somewhat foggy day.

My husband volunteered to climb a tree with the goal of spotting our lake with its campground.

Woods Lesson #2: When you climb a tree in thick woods, you see more trees; even our moderately sized lake was hidden.

"Okay," we said, "on which side of the tree is the moss growing?"

Woods Lesson #3: In cold, damp woods, the moss grows on all sides of the trees.

We then decided to follow the next stream, believing it would likely lead to a lake, which would have people around it, and a road. However, the small stream we followed soon branched. We then chose what seemed to be the main branch and followed it, but it then branched again and again.

Woods Lesson #4: Streams flow downhill and either divide or join other streams as gravity draws them all downward.

By this time, we were taking turns climbing trees to continually search for any lake. Finally, my husband spotted a lake, so we lined up in its direction, but we had to climb several more trees to keep going in the right direction.

Woods Lesson #5: Distances are hard to estimate in unfamiliar territory.

By now our feet were soaked since we had crossed more and more branching streams and were walking in the three-foot-deep water of a swamp. As the sun set, it began to rain. Our three-year-old son suddenly burst out crying and screaming because he had obviously realized his parents had no idea what they were doing and that we were all in serious trouble. While somewhat managing to calm him down, we assessed our immediate situation and agreed that first we needed to get out of the water.

We found some slightly higher ground and stumbled, exhausted, into the minimal shelter of a large, fallen tree. We were all shivering and had no jackets, sweaters, food, or matches. My husband had once seen a demonstration of starting a fire by wrapping a boot lace around a pointed stick and then twirling it on top of a piece of wood. He tried this diligently for what seemed like at least an hour or more to no avail.

Woods Lesson #6: Forget any lessons about trick ways to start fires when the wood is wet.

After giving up with the fire, we simply huddled together. Our children fell fast asleep, and my husband seemed to sleep intermittently, but I spent the longest and most sleepless night of my life. *What have we done?* I thought. *Not only have we stupidly gotten ourselves into danger; we have brought our two innocent children into it.* Even though I was and still am an atheistic agnostic, I thought, *God*—just in case someone was listening—*if you get us out of this, I will never complain about anything ever again.*

The sun finally rose on a cold and dripping woods. This created our first challenge of the day—breaking loose from the relative warmth of our tightly entangled bodies. We then began moving rapidly to warm up with the hopes of finding another of those old logging roads. The old road we finally found was now overgrown with two-foot-tall trees. Not knowing which direction to take, we arbitrarily chose one direction and planned to follow it until it either led somewhere or came to an end.

Our chosen direction soon ended at a wall of impenetrable trees, so we turned around and went the other direction, which eventually brought us to a crossroads of similarly overgrown roads. We decided that at any crossroads, we would take the one that appeared to be less overgrown. On and on we trekked, each of us with a child on his or her back, turning back at more dead ends and making decisions at more crossroads.

By then the sun had come out, and the mosquitos had begun swarming. At least, however, we were now warm and had even been able to pick some scattered blackberries. We were about to turn back on one more road, which appeared to be coming to a dead end, when I decided to go up to its very end to be sure it really ended.

Hallelujah! It wasn't a dead end. I saw a lake about ten feet through the trees … and a boathouse … and a dirt road! The two of us could barely move, but I drew on the memory of a war movie, in which a soldier struggled through a rain forest and kept repeating, "One foot in front of the other." That sentence brought us all out to an asphalt highway. I, who had always complained about "too much asphalt," was so happy to see asphalt that I was tempted to kiss it.

In a short while, a car appeared, driving slowly around a curve as my husband stuck out his thumb. The car stopped, and we were all invited to pile inside. My husband told the lone driver what had happened and the name of the campground to which we needed to return. Thank goodness he remembered the name, which I had never even noted.

Our driver was a local farmer, who told us that the

campground was about ten miles away. He then proceeded to slowly turn around on a blind curve, while I held my breath, hoping no other car was coming. Then he began to ask for more details about what had happened and where we were from. When my husband replied that we were from Milwaukee, he said, "Oh, do you know my friend, Tom?"

When my husband said, "No, we don't know him," our driver's tone rapidly changed. He turned his body (while driving) and suspiciously remarked, "You don't know Tom? He lives in Milwaukee."

Our response that Milwaukee was a big city didn't satisfy him. He said he never picked up hitchhikers and had done so only because of seeing the "woman and children." He also said that going out of his way would cost him a lot of money for gas and that if any kind of accident happened, he would have to blame it on us.

So here we were, having just escaped the woods, only to now be in a car with a paranoid and possibly dangerous man. Those ten miles back to our campground were the longest ten miles of our lives. Finally, we reached our campground, my husband threw him some money from his wallet (thank goodness, he still had his wallet), and we fled from the car into our blessed tent. The two of us fell into a deep sleep while the children, who had been carried all morning, leaped about, happily eating chocolate bars. We drove home that day. My husband went to work the next day, and I never even developed a cold.

This frightening experience occurred in the 1960s, decades before cell phones had been invented. It impressed us both deeply, and we talked about it for a long time. I insisted on retelling it to our children because I didn't want them to grow up with some sort of mysterious nightmare in the backs of their minds.

Subsequent news stories of others becoming lost and surviving or not surviving caught our attention in new ways, and we read several books on survival. I have forgotten the authors and titles of those books, but I have never forgotten the especially valuable advice provided by one author. If you think there is even a chance that you have lost your way, stop! Recognize and accept the reality of being lost. Do not continue without knowing where you are as this will likely result in you becoming more and more lost. Chances of either finding your way or of being found by others are greatly improved by stopping, marking the spot and then slowly and methodically exploring out from that known location.

Regardless of the wonderful GPS systems on cell phones today, I habitually pay attention to compass directions whether I'm walking or driving. I'm aware that it's still possible to suddenly walk or drive into areas with poor cell phone reception and that cell phone batteries function poorly in temperatures at or below freezing.

Chapter 28

MAROONED FOR A NIGHT

Like most of us, I had heard the warnings about not swimming or boating alone, but one summer day in the late 1970s, I really wanted to sail and no one else wanted to join me. I rationalized that I would only be boating on a lake; there would be lots of other people and boats around, and I was a strong swimmer.

I hauled my small boat to Lake Houston, the water reservoir about twenty miles north of Houston. (I said it was a "small boat," but it was barely a real boat; it was a Styrofoam board with a shallow sitting area and a single sail hanging on an aluminum mast.) I sailed out into the lake on a calm day among lots of other boaters. I was a beginning sailor, however, and the boat had only one sail, so it wasn't easy for me to navigate, and the boat tended to tip over whenever a strong gust of wind caught the sail. Although righting the boat was manageable with my own body weight leaning back and pulling from the opposite side, it was a challenge.

After a couple of hours, I was becoming tired of constantly having to haul up that water-filled sail, and I noticed all the other boats heading for the dock. I heeded this warning and turned toward the dock at the south end of the lake. The wind was against me, but I had recently had a lesson in tacking—that is, sailing at a forty-five-degree angle against the wind. I attempted this type of maneuvering, but as a beginner with just one sail, I simply ended up sailing horizontally to the wind back and forth across the lake.

After numerous additional episodes of tipping, hauling up the sail, and righting the boat, the mast broke. Now I had one dangling sail, the sun was beginning to set, I was exhausted, and all the other boats were back at the dock and out of signaling distance.

I decided I couldn't simply keep going back and forth across the lake in the dark. I needed to land somewhere somehow. Rather than fight the wind, I turned the boat downwind. In that instant, the wind caught my half sail, and suddenly I was flying into the north shore of the lake, afraid I would be injured or even killed. Amazingly, I landed without a scratch, probably due to the weeds and small branches that slowed the boat.

There I was in my bathing suit with no shoes, no shirt, and no food as darkness fell. Fortunately, it was summer, and I sort of liked the image and adventure of wrapping up in my sail for the night and solving the problem in the morning. Before wrapping up, I studied my surroundings and noticed that although there were houses on the lake's other shores, there were none on my shore.

On my shore, I saw only trees, bushes, and a small meadow where about half a dozen horses were grazing. I was very tired, though, so I wrapped up in my sail and settled in behind some bushes. I became only slightly annoyed when I had to pull the sail over my face as protection from the mosquitoes. I slept lightly, occasionally awakened by the sounds of the horses. I even had an interesting dream, in which I was sleeping under bushes next to a road in which a procession of medieval English royalty was passing.

The next morning I tried to repair the broken mast using various branches and other items, but alas, there was nothing with which to tie them securely. After a few unsuccessful sailing attempts, I tried plan B, which was to paddle, but again there was no suitable material, and I simply ended up paddling furiously with no detectable progress.

I then considered plan C, which was to leave my boat and begin walking around the lake back to the park. This seemed feasible since I could see the dock in the distance. Since I had no shoes, I thought, *Feet, be tough*! and began walking slowly and gingerly over dirt, twigs, and rocks. After about an hour of this walking, I spied a lost flip-flop sandal. What a treasure!

With one foot now protected, I continued walking along the edge of the lake until I encountered a swampy area. *Uh-oh*, I thought, *there are likely to be alligators and snakes in there, so I'd better find a way around it*. I then began walking perpendicular (north) away from the lake and walked and walked until I saw a large rock, on which I sat down to rest.

After a few minutes, I continued walking and finally estimated that I might be far enough north of the lake to turn westward, following the sun, and then turn back southward toward the lake, thus bypassing the swampy area. After more walking, I glimpsed a clearing through the trees and optimistically approached it, but it was the same clearing and the same rock on which I had sat an hour or more earlier. I had often read about people walking in circles when lost in the woods and couldn't understand how that could happen, but now I had done it.

Arriving at that same rock was indeed discouraging, but I had no choice other than to attempt to regain my bearings and again walk north away from the lake and again turn to follow the sun in a westward direction and again walk southward back toward the lake. This time I reached the lake on the other side of the swamp. Whew!

All I had to do then was climb up and over some cliffs to reach what appeared to be houses and backyards. While climbing, I found another treasure, a large rubber shoe, which I happily added to my other foot. I must have looked a little odd with two oversized shoes of different types, but I no longer had to take turns protecting one foot or the other.

Finally, I found a driveway, where I was able to walk out on a beautiful asphalt road. I walked along until a man in a pickup truck pulled up and asked whether I needed any help. Although I had always feared getting into any vehicle with a stranger, I thought, *This is a time to accept a ride from a stranger. If he is dangerous, I'll deal with that later.* He wasn't dangerous, though; he was simply someone doing a good deed, and I arrived back at my car in a short time.

I had kept my car keys all this time, so I simply got in and drove back home. I called my office, where they expressed relief to hear from me since they had been calling all morning. (Note: cell phones hadn't yet been invented in the 1970s.) I then ate and drank something and collapsed, exhausted, into my bed.

I returned to the lake a few days later, and someone with a motorboat took me to recover my boat. It was gone, however, and all I could think was, *good riddance. The next time I get in a boat, it had better be seaworthy!* Although I had been marooned for only one night, I had learned much from the decision-making, fear, courage, and toughness I had needed during those few hours. Also, I do believe that was the last time I went swimming or boating alone.

Chapter 29

SUPPER ON THE BEACH

At over sixty miles long, Padre Island National Seashore is the longest stretch of undeveloped barrier island in the world.[25] It lies just off the coast of southern Texas and northern Mexico and east of Corpus Christi. Its eastern side, known as Laguna Madre, is a major seagrass ecosystem for crabs, birds, and other sea life.[26]

One evening, while walking along the Padre Island surf, I suddenly realized the colors of the sunset were being reflected in the wet sand at my feet. As I watched in awe, the colors became even more intense. I rubbed my eyes, refocused, and then saw that those intense colors were due to the appearance of millions of tiny, multicolored, irides-cent seashells working their way up through the wet sand. By tiny, I mean about as big as the end of my little finger. I had often seen them in the past and didn't pay them much attention—individually they seemed so inconsequential. Yet in the millions, they formed an unforgettable sight.

Simultaneously, I heard a strange clicking sound filling the air. Scanning my surroundings, I discovered its source—an army of crabs marching out of the surf. They were scooping up those tiny shells and grinding them into even tinier pieces, which were cascading down from the sides of their mouths. *Crabs!* I thought. *It's time to go crabbing!* I hurried to tell my family and friends. We grabbed nets, ran back to the surf, and hauled in crabs as fast as we could. Someone yelled, "Throw back the egg-bearing females!"

We had a memorable supper of crabs boiled in seawater. Cleanup was even provided courtesy of the seagulls who ate the leftovers. *Wow!* I marveled. *We just fell into a food chain.* What a privilege to have been part of this amazing web of life! It was all so easy with every player doing his or her part. The tiny, sea-shelled ones had eaten microscopic organisms on grains of sand and then been eaten by crabs, who were eaten by humans and finally by seagulls. I had stumbled into this supper event at just the right time—low tide, which had exposed the seafloor, sunset, which had awakened hungry crabs, humans who noted the crabs, and finally seagulls patrolling in the air.

I later learned that those tiny shells were coquina (*Donax variabilis texasiana*), a type of mollusk.[27] A park ranger confirmed this and said the crabs were likely blue crabs (*Callinectes sapidus*). He also said that in the 1970s, a coquina chowder was often served on the menu at the park visitor center and employee potlucks.[28] (In recent years, I have seen only scattered clusters of coquinas, unlikely to be sufficient for chowder.)

Conservation of tiny coquina mollusks can aid in the conservation of the blue crab. It begins by not driving on wet
sand exposed at low tide, which can kill or damage millions
of them and not over enthusiastically collecting them for
jewelry. Similarly important is the preservation of the coastal
marshes where blue crabs breed.[29]

Part Eight

GLIMPSES INTO A
FEW TRADITIONS

Chapter 30

DREAMING YOM KIPPUR

One night I dreamed thousands of other people and I were working as slaves in a large factory somewhere in Europe. Suddenly, we found ourselves standing on the banks of a wide river and singing a joyful song in Hebrew. I woke up just in time to hear the news on the radio that this day was Yom Kippur.

What did this mean that I had that dream on that day? Had my subconscious somehow tapped into an underlying human consciousness, as described by Karl Jung?[30] Had my knowledge and feelings concerning the Holocaust been stuck in my subconsciousness for decades and simply burst forth on that morning? Was this a remnant of the songs accompanying Hebrew folk dances of our Houston International Folkdance group?[31] Was the timing synchronous or pure coincidence? I have no idea.

Regardless of this strange coincidence, I subsequently spent some time learning about the holiday of Yom Kippur. Despite my early Catholic religious training, I had always been curious about Judaism and felt drawn to many of its teachings. Yom Kippur means "Day of Atonement," and it follows the ten days of Rosh Hashanah, which are devoted to self-examination and penance for actions during the past year.[32]

I don't know the details of what prayers are said on Yom Kippur or how practitioners examine their actions of the past year, but this concept led me to think about other religious and cultural practices involving an examination of past actions. I was familiar with confession in the Catholic church of my youth, in which I confessed to a priest, who then assigned a certain number of prayers to be said as punishment. Although it was said to wipe my soul clean so I "wouldn't go to hell in the afterlife," I never really learned anything from it, such as how to act differently in the future. I also couldn't understand how it would benefit anyone else who might have been harmed by whatever sin I had committed.

During the rite of Communion in the Episcopal Church, members examine their lives, acknowledge sins before God, and prepare to make restitution for all injuries and wrongs done to others. They also forgive others who have offended them. If any people need help and counsel, they have the option of confessing to a priest.[33]

The Baha'i faith is a religion that grew out of the Islamic religion and culture of Iraq in the early 1800s. Members believe all souls are equal; accordingly, they don't have priests and confess only to God. Confession to another person isn't permitted although they may apologize to the person wronged.[34]

Examples in the secular world also exist. Alcoholics Anonymous (AA) specifies "taking a moral inventory of ourselves" and "admitting to God, to ourselves, and to another human being the exact nature of our wrongs," as the fourth and fifth steps of the twelve steps to recovery from alcoholism.[35] Acknowledging past actions with a professional counselor is a current practice that may lead to reconciliation and the atonement of broken relationships.

My personal review of the previous year usually occurs at the New Year and takes the form of an annual letter to family and friends. It's not a confession since it typically tells an upbeat story of my past year's travels and accomplishments, but it does serve as a memory device that sometimes brings up past actions, of which I am not so proud.

Past failings or "sins" can be complex, however. Some sins or failings would seem to be obvious, such as lying, cheating, stealing, adultery, or murder. Yet even these supposedly obvious examples have their exceptions, such as killing in self-defense or lying to save your life when captured in a time of war. Consider also that adultery was incorporated into the Ten Commandments at a time when men could have multiple wives. During my childhood, disobeying parents was regarded as a sin to be confessed. In adulthood, however, some would regard disobeying or rebelling against a government (in the role of a parent) to be a heroic act.

I have never purposely sought to hurt anyone, yet there have been times when pursuing my own path has been hurtful to others. Of course, examination of how one might act to inflict the least amount of harm on another should be encouraged before one commits the act. I can recall times in past decades of office work when some of my coworkers and I gossiped about others, a sin in the Baha'i religion. Perhaps this could have been avoided by directly confronting those who were the object of gossip because of what were perceived to be their negative behaviors. On the other hand, sometimes direct confrontations are rebuffed so people understandably turn to others for a resolution of interpersonal problems. And what about mental illness? Or just confusion that harms other people?

The more I thought about the whole concept of failings and sin or at least responsibility, the more complex it seemed. In any case, Judaism takes confession a step further by requiring atonement on Yom Kippur. *Atonement* typically has two definitions: "reparation" (repair or making amends) for an offense or injury and "reconciliation" (restoration to friendship or harmony). [36] Atonement goes beyond simply confessing and repairing your soul; it requires deep thought and practical steps to repair damage done to others.

One often hears of reparations demanded by the victors after a war. At the end of World War I, for example, the victors (France, Britain, and the United States) required reparations from the remaining central powers. However, the only remaining central power with a relatively intact economy was Germany, so it effectively had to pay all the reparations. This wasn't a true example of atonement, since it wasn't what the German people had independently decided to do, but rather it was a penalty imposed on them. It caused enormous suffering and resentment and many considered it to be one of the roots of World War II.[37,38]

Reparations were again required of Germany at the end of World War II, to be paid to both the victors and to the Jewish survivors of the Holocaust. However, numerous adjustments were made in recognition that complete destitution would adversely affect other European countries and that Germany had now been divided into two parts between the Soviet Union and the Western powers.[39]

And what about atonement for almost two hundred years of slavery and subsequent discrimination against black people in the United States? At the end of the Civil War in the United States, General Sherman proposed that freed slaves be given forty-acre parcels of land along the East Coast, from Charleston, South Carolina, to the St. Johns River in Florida. President Lincoln approved his order, but President Andrew Johnson overturned it less than a year later.[40] How can centuries of pain and suffering be redeemed? The issue is still being debated.[41]

An act of atonement occurred in 1988 when the US Congress and the president acknowledged the injustice of placing American citizens of Japanese descent in concentration camps during World War II. They paid reparations of $20,000 to each survivor.[42]

Another act of atonement occurred in 1994 at the end of apartheid in South Africa. A Truth and Reconciliation Commission was formed to investigate human rights abuses that had taken place, and once identified, they were referred to a Reparation and Rehabilitation Committee "to ensure non repetition, healing and healthy co-existence."[43]

Thus, the uncanny occurrence of a dream on Yom Kippur unexpectedly led me to dig further into questions of self-examination and atonement on both individual and societal levels. What is an individual's responsibility for the actions of his or her society? What if one hasn't committed anything unjust but simply inherited ill-gotten benefits from previous generations? How does one extricate himself or herself from unjust portions of society and atone for damages created from such tangled webs?

Questions concerning atonement, with its elements of reparation and reconciliation, remain especially relevant today in the United States. Cries of "Black Lives Matter" make it evident that past and current acts of injustice must be addressed since they don't simply disappear.

Chapter 31

FASTING FOR RAMADAN

One of the Islamic religious practices that the Baha'is continued was fasting at Ramadan. Within Islam, Ramadan occurs according to a lunar calendar, which varies from year to year so periods of fasting occur on days of varying lengths. The Baha'is, however, modified the practice by following a solar calendar, in which they observed Ramadan only at the spring equinox, when the hours of daylight fasting were always equal to the number of hours of nighttime feasting.[44]

After listening to my husband's explanation of the health and spiritual benefits of such modified yearly fasting, I decided to try it for myself. The difference between my husband's practice and mine was that I was a vegetarian, while he was an omnivore. Each morning before dawn, he ate a breakfast of three eggs, sausage, potatoes, toast, orange juice, and coffee. I ate a bowl of whole-grain cereal with fruit and nuts plus a cup of tea. He then rode a bike to his job, where he worked at a desk, while I rode a bike to my studio, where I did massage.

Each afternoon, I was so hungry that I was barely able to function. One afternoon, I was so hungry that I decided that vegetables and grain would simply not be adequate and that I would need to eat some meat at sundown. There was a highly rated barbecue restaurant around the corner from my studio, so my thoughts immediately zeroed in on it. I wasn't salivating for beef but rather for their barbecue duck, which I had eaten in my previous omnivore years.

The more I anticipated that plate of roasted duck, the stronger my hunger became. Suddenly, a worry occurred to me. *What if the restaurant no longer serves duck?* Or *what if they have simply run out of the day's supply?* This worry wouldn't let me go, and I began to think of alternatives. There were no other restaurants I knew of within biking distance that served duck, and I wasn't ready to compromise by eating beef. What else could I do?

Then I remembered that live ducks were swimming around in a nearby park. I could go and choke one of those ducks, butcher it, cook it and eat it. *What?* I, the vegetarian, was planning to slaughter a duck with my bare hands? Then I recognized that a deep hunter-killer instinct had awakened within my body and soul. That led me to think about the millions of people in the world who were truly hungry. And then I thought about the depth of that hunger and the hunter-killer instincts that must awaken in most, if not all, of those people. And then I realized I had apparently learned a major lesson at Ramadan—empathy for those who are hungry and recognition of the danger of hunger's closely allied killer instincts.

Chapter 32

HEARING AN EASTER CRY

(Please note that, as in the previous chapter on prayer and yearning, the lesson I learned in this chapter is based on my own experiences and perceptions. It isn't intended to be a challenge to the beliefs of others, who have had different experiences and perceptions.)

As stated in the Bible, "Jesus cried with a loud voice, saying My God, my God, why hast thou forsaken me." (Mathew 26:46 and Mark 15:34). (These and other statements from the Bible are from the King James Version, but similar statements may be found in other versions). This is the voice I have heard from the cross every Easter throughout my childhood and part of my adulthood. It disturbed me then, and it disturbs me now— someone alone, desperate, and in pain.

"For God so loved the world, that he gave his only begotten son, that whosoever believeth in him shall not perish, but have everlasting life." (John 3:16) Really? As a child, I doubted this message; as an adult, I do not believe it. I have simply not been able to accept the idea that the torture of someone over two thousand years ago somehow redeemed or "saved" me or anyone else from our sins. What I have heard and do believe is that Jesus was in pain.

Rather than being comforted or grateful for the sacrifice of Jesus on the cross, I continue to be deeply disturbed by the cruelty of other human beings. I recognize that many ancient cultures sacrificed both humans and animals from Abraham of the Old Testament, who was ready to kill his own son, (Genesis 22:1–13) to Aztec peoples sacrificing young couples.[45] Such practices seem forgivable for prior ages when the origins of droughts, floods, storms, and famines were thought to be due to wrathful gods, but not today.

Although the verse from John appears to attribute the crucifixion of Jesus to God, other New Testament verses tell of humans who shared responsibility: religious and civil authorities who judged that Jesus had broken the law. (Mathew 27:1–26) What law? Does it matter? If someone has broken a law, it would have been his or her mind that directed his or her mouth, hands, or other part of his or her body to break that law. So why punish the physical body?

Why should punishments for breaking any laws be so cruel? Authorities often cite the deterrence of future lawbreakers as a rationalization for cruel punishments. How effective is this? The crucifixion of Jesus probably scared many people into silence, but his teachings grew anyway. Even the cruelty inflicted on multitudes of early Roman Christian martyrs failed to stem the growth of this new religion. I wonder what proportion of the non-Christian citizens of Rome felt "protected" by those executions. In our times, I haven't felt "protected" when agents of my government have used "enhanced interrogation" to wring information out of prisoners of war.

In short, Easter isn't my time to feel grateful for "everlasting life" brought about by the torture of anyone. Because I had never heard anyone else express anything like my abhorrence of this tradeoff for everlasting life, I supposed or at least wondered whether I might be the only one in all these centuries to feel this way.

I asked our Unitarian-Universalist minister, and she responded by recommending the book *Proverbs of Ashes*. This book let me know I wasn't alone in the horror I had experienced concerning the torture of the crucifixion. The two authors also alerted me to a connection I hadn't previously considered: victims of abuse who suffer in silence in their attempts to be like Jesus. Some of the authors' key points were:

➢ "Rather than being a spiritual gift, the crucifixion of Jesus was a public execution performed by an oppressive empire.

➢ It's wrong to confuse hate with love.

➢ How can Christianity promise healing to victims when a divine parent has required the death of his child?

➢ The self-sacrifice of Jesus on the cross did not end dominance and submission; his death was a consequence of domination, not its cure.

➤ Any distinction between voluntary and involuntary suffering confuses matters; in each case the perpetrator remains the same.

➤ Love does not require that we sacrifice our safety or self-respect." [46]

Several governmental organizations have renounced torture. The US Constitution declares, "Excessive bail shall not be required, nor excessive fines imposed, nor cruel and unusual punishments inflicted."[47] The Universal Declaration of Human Rights declares, "No one shall be subjected to torture or to cruel, inhuman or degrading treatment or punishment."[48] The Geneva Convention states, "No physical or mental torture may be inflicted on prisoners of war to secure from them information of any kind whatever." [49] The European Convention on Human Rights states, "No one shall be subjected to torture or to inhuman or degrading treatment or punishment."[50]

Where are the churches in denouncing torture? How about introducing a new Easter theme—an acknowledgment and expression of regret for the suffering of Jesus and the many other people who have been tortured? At least one national or international prohibition against torture could be read at that time.

Part Nine

EXPANDING HORIZONS

Chapter 33

TRAVELS IN TIME AND SPACE

When I was in college, I took a few classes in other languages, but never pictured myself as having the funds or opportunities to travel to other countries. This was short-sighted thinking as I never foresaw how much more efficient and economical travel would become in the next decades. Although my trips have only been for weeks at a time, traveling seemed to expand time as all my senses seemed to become more alive and focused.

Traveling beyond my comfortable boundaries has broadened my perceptions of life in unexpected ways. Unexpected observations and encounters have occurred beyond the different sounds, scenery, museums, and foods of other cultures. Although I've loved these forays into other lands and cultures, I've also loved journeying back to familiar places to see what has happened in intervening decades.

Manhattan Island

As a child, I had love-hate feelings about the city of New York. On the one hand, I loved visiting my grandmother, who lived on the East Side, a block from where the new building for the UN was being built. I also loved visiting the Museum of Natural History, where I spent hours while my parents shopped, and I loved visits to the theater.

On the other hand, I was always afraid of getting lost, and since we didn't own a car, I had never seen a travel map. I especially hated the city's heat, grime, and pollution. Those were the days before air conditioning when everyone smoked. Riding in a New York City taxicab or train, in which the uphol-stery was saturated with cigarette smoke, made me nauseous.

After my family and I moved from the New York City area in 1956, I never missed it, but I was always interested in its history. One of the characteristics of the city that had particularly mystified me was why it was so flat when the surrounding area was so hilly. I later learned in a PBS television special that, in fact, the island of Manhattan had also once been hilly. It had been literally flattened in the late 1800s so engineers could construct a gridiron of streets.

In 1994, I had a reason to travel through the city. Although I was curious to see it again after forty years, I felt the return of my childhood fears of getting lost and especially dreaded the poor air quality. This time, though, I bought a map and had no problems finding my way across the city. I was really surprised, though, by the air quality, which was better than what I was breathing in Houston. New York City now had air conditioning, no smoking on taxis or mass transit, and improved exhaust systems, while Houston had millions of cars and surrounding oil refineries.

Oklahoma

During my four years in the late 1950s at the University of Oklahoma, I was on the women's synchronized swim team. We practiced in a pool, which was about the size of an average living room. Our only public recognition was on Mother's Day weekend when we performed for our visiting mothers. Meanwhile, the men's swim team practiced in an Olympic-sized pool and had scholarships, special T-shirts, and extensive public recognition in the Olympics and other events.

When I returned for my fortieth reunion of my college class in 2000, our small women's pool had been drained and turned into a miniature canyon with suitable plantings. Everyone on campus now had access to Olympic-sized indoor and outdoor pools, athletic scholarships, and other benefits. This was due to the passage of the Title IX law in 1972. (Before 1972, one in twenty-seven girls played sports; by 2016, that number was two in five.) Title IX states, "No person in the United States shall, on the basis of sex, be excluded from participation in, be denied the benefits of, or be subjected to discrimination under any educational program or activity receiving Federal financial assistance."[51]

My first drive into western Oklahoma had been in 1956 with my future husband on the way to meet his family. They lived on a farm west of the cities of Fort Sill and Lawton. This was the first time I had driven onto the plains of Oklahoma, and I felt like we were driving off into space.

I loved meeting his family, who were so welcoming and interesting. I quickly discovered, however, that rather than joining in with the farm work of plowing and herding cattle, I was expected to join the farm work of cooking and cleaning up after the large meals. Although I could see the value of both sides of farm work, I really wanted to be outdoors, doing the kinds of work I had been reading about and watching in movies; either that or in the living room telling stories and arguing with the men about politics. The end of every meal was an internal struggle, in which my desires competed with my responsibilities to support the cleanup operations. Although I loved this family, I was constantly at odds with them over my role.

When I returned for a visit forty years later, the pattern was pretty much the same. There had, however, been a slight shift in attitudes, since I was no longer seen as the odd one, and some of the men occasionally helped with cleanup. My now-former husband had even told me about one of the granddaughters who had been very much like me in wanting to fully engage in the outdoor work of the farm. I appreciated the generosity of spirit he must have had to be able to share that with me. My former father-in-law even accepted my offer to help him hand-weed one of the cotton patches. While weeding, he said, "You know, I actually admired you." No matter how late, that recognition really felt good.

West Texas

On a trip to far West Texas, I found an unexpected solution to a missed bus departure. Not wanting to drive over six hundred miles each way by myself, I had taken the overnight train from Houston to the small town of Alpine, where I planned to board a bus for the oasis campground of Balmorhea State Park. However, the train was delayed for several hours, and by the time it reached Alpine, I had missed the last bus to Balmorhea. As I stood there, wondering what to do, a man got out of an unmarked car and asked where I was going. When I told him Balmorhea, he offered to drive me the fifty miles for fifty dollars and assured me that he routinely did this for people.

"Sorry," I said, "there's no way that I will get into an unmarked car with a strange man."

I had limited money, though, so I didn't want to spend it on one of the hotels in town, which would have cost a lot more. I thought about it some more and realized that in a town the size of Alpine, someone must know him. I asked the ticket clerk of the bus company about him. She didn't personally know him, but she called her cousin at the bank, who did know and recommend him. My ride to Balmorhea with this recommended stranger was delightful, since he had lived in the area for decades and was also a tour guide at Big Bend National Park. The fifty miles sped by as he told me stories about the history of the land and ranches along our route.

My second surprise was that August was rainy season in West Texas. (I didn't know it even had a rainy season.) As I was setting up my tent, black clouds gathered, the sky darkened, and a strong wind threatened to blow my tent away as large raindrops pelted me. I dove into my tent, where I huddled for the next hour, hoping I wouldn't be flooded. Suddenly, the rain stopped, and the sun came out.

I heard a woman's voice say, "Well, that was something!" and I met the woman who had the next campsite. She invited me to share supper with her and told me she was from Austin; we were instantly compatible. She then asked whether I would like to join her on a trip to see the "mystery lights of Marfa." I had never heard of such a thing, so of course I said yes.

We got into her pickup truck and began driving southward over the same fifty miles I had traveled that afternoon. Again, it rained and threatened to wash us off the road, but we made it to the town of Marfa and obtained directions on where to watch for the mystery lights.

No one seems to know why these lights appear in the air over certain areas. Various theories involving gases, military exercises, and UFOs have been discredited. We, however, never saw anything due to the dense fog from the recent heavy rains.

Years later, I returned to Marfa with friends and did see some lights. They looked to me like distant yard lights or trucks on a highway, but I was assured that their location indicated that they were the mystery lights.

China

When I went on a bicycle tour in China in 1982, as expected, I saw many people doing Tai Chi and other exercises in the parks. What I had not expected to see were daily examples of the strength of the Chinese people. While our group pedaled along on lightweight multi-geared bicycles, those around us kept pace with old and heavy bicycles with no gears. Many of them also carried a baby, toddler, spouse or groceries. I saw old ladies hauling carts of bricks and even cement blocks. One morning, I watched a woman rapidly walking along while carrying two buckets of melons, one hanging from each side of a shoulder yoke. That, alone, was impressive, but one of the buckets also held a seated toddler.

That was almost 40 years ago when private individuals in China did not own cars. The few vehicles on the road were owned by government agencies, factories or tour groups. Most of the vehicles on the road were bicycles. Now that China has joined most of the rest of the world in converting to cars, I wonder what has happened to all that impressive strength.

(Additional experiences in China are described in Chapter 13, Swinging Between Nutrition Concepts and Chapter 23, Trading Cars with China and Other Economic Lessons.)

Northern Europe

A couple of years after my trip to China, I had an opportunity for a bicycle trip with my male companion through the countries of Germany, Denmark, and Sweden. Our first stop was the city of Hamburg, Germany, which I expected to be a large, crowded, cold, and gray industrial city. To my surprise, it was sunny, clean, and beautiful. It had wide streets, beautiful parks, outdoor cafés, flowers, and street music. It even had special traffic lanes with signals for cyclists.

Although we were there in the middle of the week, crowds of people were out enjoying the parks and sidewalk cafés. Somewhat mystified, I asked our bed-and-breakfast hostess why no one seemed to be at work. "Oh," she said, "this is August when most Europeans vacation; those who are now working, such as waiters and tour guides, vacationed in July."

The atmosphere felt so light, relaxed, and joyful that I began letting go of the stress of my job and trip preparations. The thought dawned on me that perhaps a major portion of the health problems in our own country was due to our lack of sufficient vacation time.

When we traveled through the countryside of northern Germany, all the roads and intersections were carefully marked, and we never once saw any litter, which fulfilled the predictions I had heard.

In one small town, I encountered something unexpected, although it shouldn't have been unexpected. As I stood before a memorial to the sons of townspeople who had died in the war, I felt my usual sadness at the loss of such young lives. Then I had another thought. *These were Nazi soldiers.* But then I quickly had another thought. *It doesn't matter; they probably had little or no choice in going to war, and the hurt their families and loved ones felt would have been the same as that felt by anyone in any country.*

We left the town of Lubeck on a mammoth ferry bound for Denmark. As we were disembarking on our bicycles, huge semitrucks roared past us into the distance. Suddenly it was quiet, and we saw that we were in a village of about a dozen houses with a divided bicycle highway in front of us. We cycled on it through fields of golden grain with the sun beginning to set. Just as it was getting dark, we came upon another cluster of small houses with a restaurant and a filling station.

Small villages with small houses, small restaurants, small roads, and small cars were the pattern all along our way for three days until we reached Copenhagen. Occasional train crossings had signs that indicated what appeared to be toy trains, and sure enough, the trains were short, quiet, and painted red. Everything was so small and toylike that I felt like Gulliver in the land of the Lilliputians. Then it occurred to me that perhaps the houses and other objects in Denmark weren't unusually small; perhaps they were just more human sized than what I was used to in the United States, where people enjoyed the luxury of lots of space in which to build big.

By the time we reached Sweden, I had become used to smaller houses and dedicated bicycle highways, but I wasn't accustomed to gray skies, rain, and cold weather—in August. One day we cycled for seventy miles through cold, driving rain. *Hmm,* I thought. *No wonder so many people emigrated to the Americas!*

One evening, as we cycled back from one of the beautiful island parks of Stockholm, my bare legs began to freeze in the sudden cold wind. "Turn here," said my companion, and we turned onto a street in the Old Town, which was only wide enough for a single file of pedestrians. Suddenly the wind stopped, and it was warm. *Oh,* I thought, *that's why the streets from the Middle Ages in Europe are so narrow; they offer protection from the cold wind.*

Travels in countries where one doesn't know the language can be intimidating, but I have been amazed by how many people in other countries speak more than one language, especially English. I've also found that it helps to at least learn some of the basics of the other language, such as "Where is the hotel? Bus? Bathroom? How much does this cost?"

Sweden was a challenge, though, because the Swedes were so accomplished in other languages. I often began a sentence in Swedish, only to have it finished for me in English. My companion, who had grown up in Sweden, explained, "Ours is such a small country that we knew no one would bother to learn Swedish, so we had to learn their languages."

Peru

On a trip to Machu Pichu in Peru, I was shocked to see people in the mountains living in one-room stone houses with no electricity or plumbing and only an open fire at one end. Yet the women were quite wealthy in terms of their intricately woven clothing of many colors. I could only imagine how much time and skill must have been required to make such beautiful and rich textiles.

And what strong people they were to live at these altitudes above ten thousand feet with cheeks that were permanently red, which were apparently related to their super-efficient oxygen utilization. One day as our group collapsed in a state of exhaustion on the side of a mountain peak, we noticed a child, who must have been about two years old watching us from another mountain peak. We watched as he ran with his little legs down the side of his mountain, across the bridge of a stream, and up the side of our mountain. He stared at us for a few minutes and then ran back home.

Italy

On a trip to Italy in 2019, I was surprised that Rome still had not only many of its ancient buildings at least partially standing but also had its ancient system of public drinking fountains still providing safe drinking water. Several times I was amazed to hear operatic singing—not within opera houses but out on the streets by ordinary workmen. Also surprising to me was the fact that even dense, urban spaces appeared to be surrounded by garden plots and that the marketplaces sold a large proportion of locally or regionally made products such as paintings, pottery, and leather goods.

Mexico

Although I had been to Mexico in the early 1970s, I hadn't returned due to tales of drug wars and my previous horrible stomach and intestinal upsets. My second husband persuaded me to return with bicycles in 1992, and I was relieved not to experience any upset. Possibly this was related to the beautiful, little town of Papantla in the eastern mountains and partly to my not eating anything that wasn't cooked.

In 2015 I was again invited to travel to Mexico. This time I was more fearful of gang-related murders and kidnappings. In my debate about the wisdom of going, I considered three factors: First, I would be traveling and staying with the mother of my Spanish teacher, who had become my friend. Second, the United States itself wasn't that safe since mass shootings had recently happened in a church in Texas and a synagogue in Pennsylvania. Third, it has always been hard for me to turn down an opportunity.

Off we went by way of three buses, which took us a day and a half to reach the city of Morelia. This city of over a million people, founded in the 1500s, is situated about halfway between Mexico City and the Pacific Coast.

My first surprise occurred when I met the rest of the family at the bus station. I suddenly felt a young boy grab my suitcase, so I hung on with all my might. I wasn't going to be the victim of theft as soon as I had arrived. Then I noticed my friend's family laughing and realized, to my embarrassment, that it was their grandson trying to help by carrying my suitcase.

Like many homes in Mexico, their home blended in with the other homes on the edge of the sidewalk. It was situated over a store with the only entrance being a heavy garage door and gate. The inside was beautifully tiled with artwork and natural light from many directions.

The next day, still on my guard against theft and worse, I boarded the first of many public minibuses and was greeted by "*Buenas dias*" or "*Buen dia*" from the rest of the passengers. I then learned that the customary way of paying the fare was to hand it to the nearest passenger, who passed it along to the next one and eventually to the driver, who then passed any change due back by the same method.

Hmm, I thought. *For a country that is supposed to be full of robbers and killers, these are trusting people.* My next surprise occurred when I noticed a young man on the bus holding a mop. I supposed he had just bought it and was bringing it home to his mother. Then I saw two more young people climb on the bus with mops. Now I was mystified. The mystery was solved when they all got off the bus and joined thousands of other young people, who were cleaning the streets assisted by a truck spraying water.

I have studied Spanish on and off for many years and can get around in a Spanish-speaking country. Occasionally, however, my limited knowledge and subconscious stereotypes have led me to jump to the wrong conclusions. Once, I was traveling on a train in Mexico when I saw a man board the train and promptly begin a speech to the rest of the passengers. He became more and more agitated as he waved his arms and shouted. Then many of the other passengers began asking him questions, and some approached him either singly or in twos or threes. I was sure that he must be proposing a revolution or some major political event. Finally, I asked the woman next to me. She smiled and replied, "He is selling medicine for corns and bunions!"

What has most often amazed me during my travels has been the willingness of people in all kinds of places to help regardless of language differences. This was especially appreciated in Mexico in the late 1970s when my mother broke her hip and I had to bring her back to Houston. The help provided by so many different people on the ground, in the airports, and on the airplane dramatically convinced me that there are no unimportant jobs or people.

Chapter 34

LIGHT AND DARK

I love the light, but I also love the dark and have grown weary of light being constantly used as a metaphor for good with dark as a metaphor for bad. "I've seen the light," the song goes, but I've also seen the dark and love the darkness of my nighttime bedroom and black velvet and ebony wood and black skin and black eyes and black fur. In our culture, we have traditionally worn black at funerals, but Chinese people have traditionally worn white to symbolize skeletons.

Both light and dark have their place in our world, but too much of either can be dangerous. My blue eyes, with their lack of pigment, are more sensitive to light than those with dark eyes. Bright light causes me to squint, and I'm subject to insomnia in the spring and summer when longer hours of sunshine counteract the melatonin that would otherwise bring on sleep. I love the feeling of sunshine on my skin, but I am now having to have annual surgical removals of basal cell carcinomas from a lifetime of too much sun exposure on my pale skin.

I have been told that light is preferred because we can see in it, but our eyes also need rest. Similarly, we value our hearing, but our ears also need rest from loud or constant noise. I've been told that people fear the dark because they cannot see the danger that might be lurking there, but darkness itself can be protective.

I, like many women, was warned at an early age not to walk alone on the streets at night, but I like walking alone, and I like walking at night. I gradually rebelled against these warnings and thought, *What's the point of living in a supposedly free country if I am not free to walk at night?* So I do walk at night, but when I do, I avoid the light and walk in the shadows. Walking in protective shadows means that my eyes can adjust to the darkness and that I will be less visible to others who might be a threat.

The English language commonly associates the color black with evil as in a black heart, blacklists, black markets, and blackmail; but the color black has also been associated with power and strength as in black panthers and black belts. Our current cultural divide concerning people with different physical characteristics, immigration, and how to finance the needs of our society has been described by some as "dark." Does this mean it doesn't contain any light or understanding?

Some say this divide is a continuation of unresolved issues from the Civil War; others have noted that fear of other people and fear of job loss underlie much of the anger. Many people perhaps crave simplistic answers because their brains have tired from too much complexity. Frequent explosions of warfare provide too much light and sound rather than quiet darkness. In time, we *may see the light,* but we may also see the benefit of darkness as we learn better ways to resolve conflicts.

One Halloween night back in the 1990s, I chose to ride my bike along the dark, winding trail of Buffalo Bayou, which led directly into downtown Houston. I was on my way to a performance of the Houston Ballet, dressed as a witch with a broomstick taped to my bike. As I sped along through the shadows of trees, bushes, and underpasses, I'll admit that I was just a little scared. Then suddenly, I had to laugh as I realized I was now the one to fear. I had now become one of the scary witches of my early-childhood nightmares. Then I was speeding along through the lights of downtown and hearing pedestrians shout, "Go, Brunhilda!" The image of the scary witch had finally evolved into a beloved cartoon character.

Chapter 35

STEPPING AND DANCING

There were advantages and disadvantages to living on the fifth floor of my childhood apartment home. The advantage was the view; we could see about fifteen miles to the skyline of New York City on the horizon. The disadvantage was that we were a long way from the ground, with a rickety elevator that sometimes got stuck between floors, an experience that was quite scary. One had to ring a bell, hoping someone would hear it and then call for a maintenance man (always a man in those days).

Due to my impatience with waiting for the elevator and the fear of breakdowns, I often climbed the five floors to our apartment. I usually felt sorry for myself, thinking, *Why couldn't I live in a house with just one or two floors, like all those normal children in my storybooks?*

Nevertheless, I got good at climbing and developed my

own special technique for going down. Going down involved leaping a few steps, grabbing the post where the stairs turned between floors, swinging around with my feet in the air, and then leaping down to the next level. For some reason, I never got hurt and loved the feeling of leaping and flying. Looking back at those stair-climbing years, I credit them for my strong legs, which enabled me to dance, climb, skate, and ski.

Decades later, I repeated those early days of stair climbing in an abbreviated version when we moved into a large, two-story house. This time, though, I was no longer a young girl with strong legs, and it was just two months following the birth of our third child. As described in Chapter 9, A Time to be Born or Not, the breakage of veins in my legs (varicose veins) had become worse with each pregnancy. I couldn't stand up without pain, aching, and the breakage of even more veins. Nevertheless, I managed to climb our stairs multiple times a day without any childhood complaints. Gradually I noticed that my legs were getting stronger and no longer ached. I give credit for those improvements to renewed stair climbing.

Stairs have occasionally appeared in my dreams. Once during a time of being overwhelmed with constantly cleaning up after other people, I dreamed myself back into our old apartment, where I was scrubbing floors, while my family and friends were dancing and having a party. In my dream thoughts, I justified this as being my role. Suddenly, I said, "I don't care if this is my role; I'm not doing it anymore!" I then flung down my scrub brush, ran out the door, and began leaping and swinging down those old-childhood stairs. On and on I leaped. Gradually it occurred to me that I should have come to the ground floor, but I saw no end or exit. *Hmmm, I thought, this isn't normal. Perhaps I am in a dream, and if I am in a dream, I can change it.* So, decades before Harry Potter did it, I simply went through the next wall, came out on the other side, and woke up feeling refreshed.

During the decades of my life when I worked in an office, I always chose the stairs over the elevators, even when I worked on the tenth floor. In the beginning, I gasped for breath but was gradually able to reach all ten floors, barely out of breath. That staircase had gray walls, no air conditioning, and no windows, so it was often dank and smelly; but I did it anyway.

After retirement, I moved to the small town of Wimberley, Texas, where my new stair-climbing exercise became a small mountain with 218 steps to the peak. What a change! In contrast to the gray and dank stairs of my previous office building, these stairs were in the fresh air with wonderful views on the way up and down. Once again, stairs became my way to maintain strength in my legs for doing all the activities I loved.

One day I realized I didn't have to confine myself to simply putting one foot in front of the other for the multiple times I was climbing that mountain. To prevent boredom from repeated climbing, I varied my climbs by stepping sideward or backward or on every other step. While progressing sideways, I realized I could even weave one foot in front or behind the other foot, and suddenly I was dancing my way up.

Notes

Part 1: In the Beginning
Chapter 2: My People and Their People

1   "You've Got to Be Carefully Taught," from *South Pacific*, music by Richard Rogers, lyrics by Oscar Hammerstein. (Opened on Broadway in 1949)

Chapter 3: The Remains of Gramatan

2   [a] "Sunset Hill" (Marker Name) on List of New York State Historic Markers in Westchester County, New York. New York Museum 2009-05-03. Archived from the original 2013-03-24. Cited on Wikipedia, last edited 17 June 2021. Accessed August 24, 2021. List of New York State Historic Markers in Westchester County, New York - Wikipedia

[2b] "Aboriginal Place Names of New York," *New York State Education Dept. Bulletin* 400 (New York, 1907) Accessed August 26, 2021. Free download available at Aboriginal place names of New York : Beauchamp, William Martin, 1830-1925 : Free Download, Borrow, and Streaming : Internet Archive

[2c] Frederic Shonnard and W.W. Spooer. *History of Westchester County, New York*, Volume I. Loschberg Deutschland (www.jazzybee-verlag.de) 1900.

Part 2: In Between
Chapter 7: The Lifeguard on Duty

3   Harriet Lerner. *The Dance of Anger: A Woman's Guide To Changing The Patterns of Intimate Relationships*. Harper Collins Publishers, (First published 1985, reprinted 2014).

4   Al-Anon Family Groups. Accessed August 25, 2021. https://al-anon. org/newcomers/how-can-i-help-my/alcoholic-spouse-or-partner/.

Part 3: The Wonders and Pitfalls of Adulthood
Chapter 8: Love, Sex, Babies, and War
5   "Feeding the New Mother" and "Cow's milk protein intolerance". La Leche League, Updated 2018, Accessed August 25, 2021. https:// www.llli.org/breastfeeding-info/.
6   "Discrimination in Housing Based Upon Familial Status". Accessed August 25, 2021. https://www.justice.gov/crt/fair-housing-act-1.

Chapter 10: History and Her Story
7   Betty Fridan, "*The Feminine Mystique* (New York: W. W. Norton, 1963).

Part 4: Eating, Drinking, and Breathing
Chapter 13: Swinging between Nutrition Concepts
8   Adelle Davis, *Let's Have Healthy Children* (Ishi Press, 2013).
9   Francis Moore Lappe', *Diet for a Small Planet* (Random House, 1985).
10   Michio Kushi, Stephen Blauer, and Wendy Esko, *The Macrobiotic Way* (Penquin, 2004).
11   Dallas M. Swallow. Genetics of Lactase Persistence and Lactose Intolerance. Annual Review of Genetics. 37:197-219. 2003.

Chapter 14: The Last Times I got Drunk (or Even a Little Tipsy)
12   *The Rubaiyat of Omar Khayyam.* First translated from Persian to English 1859 by Edward Fitzgerald (Publisher Bernard Quaritch). Many editions and translations exist.

Chapter 16: Health Research Counts
13   David A. Shephard. *John Snow, Anaesthetist to a Queen and Epidemiologist to a Nation* (Cornwall, Prince Edward Island: York Point, 1995).
14   Peter Vinten-Johansen et al., *Cholera, Chloroform, and the Science of Medicine: A Life of John Snow* (Oxford: Oxford University Press, 2003). Summary by UCLA Department of Epidemiology Accessed August

25, 2021. https://www.ph.ucla.edu/epi/snow/fatherofepidemiology.html.

15 Richard Wilhelm and Cary F. Baynes, trans. et al., *The I Ching or Book of Changes* (Bollinger Series, Princeton University Press, 1967).

Chapter 18: Muscle Memory

16 Hakomi Mindful Somatic Psychotherapy. Accessed August 25, 2021. https://hakomiinstitute.com/.

Chapter 19: Expanding Health Research

17 M. A. Richardson, N. C. Russell, T. Sanders, R. Barrett, and C. Salveson. Assessment of outcomes at alternative medicine cancer clinics: a feasibility study. *J Altern Compl Med* 2001; 7(1):19-32.

18 Nancy C. Russell, Sat-Siri Sumler, Curtiss M. Beinhorn, and Moshe A. Frenkel. "Role of Massage Therapy in Cancer Care," *J Alt Comp Med* 14, no. 2 (2008): 209–214.

19 Nancy C. Russell, Deanna M. Hoelscher, and Nicki Lowenstein. "Dietary and Weight Changes after Treatments for Lymphoma," *Nutr Cancer* 57, no. 2 (2007): 168–176.

20 N. C. Russell, D. M. Hoelscher, and N. Lowenstein N, "Patients Previously Treated for Lymphoma Consume Inadequate or Excessive Amounts of Five Key Nutrients," *J Soc Integr Oncol* 5, no. 3 (2007): 118–124.

Chapter 20: Work, Play, and Health in Retirement

21 Susan Jennings, Nancy Russell, Blair Jennings, Valerie Slee, Lisa Sterling, Mariana Castells, Peter Valent, and Cem Akin. "The Mastocytosis Society Survey on Mast Cell Disorders: Patient Experiences and Perceptions," *J Allergy Clin Immunol Pract* 2, no. 1 (2014): 70–6.

22 Nancy Russell, Susan Jennings, Blair Jennings, Valerie Slee, Lisa Sterling, Mariana Castells, Peter Valent, and Cem Akin. "The Mastocytosis Society Survey on Mast Cell Disorders: Part 2-Patient Clinical Experiences and Beyond," *J Allergy Clin Immunol Pract* 7, no. 4 (April 2019): 1157–1165.

23 Paul C. Breeding, Nancy C. Russell, and Garth L. Nicolson, "Integrative Model of Chronically Activated Immune-Hormonal Pathways

Important in the Generation of Fibromyalgia," *BJMP* 5, no. 3 (2012) a524.

Part 6: Basic Skills
Chapter 24: Measuring the Earth with a Stick
24   Carl Sagan. Chapter I, "The Shores of the Cosmic Ocean" In *Cosmos* 14 – 17 (New York: Random House, 1980).

Part 7: Lessons in Nature
Chapter 29: Supper on the Beach
25   Padre Island National Seashore Texas. Accessed August 25, 2021. http://www.nps.gov/pais/index.htm.
26   The Nature Conservancy. Places We Protect Laguna Madre Texas August 25, 2021. https://www.nature.org/en-us/get-involved/how-to-help/places-we-protect/laguna-madre/.
27   Jean Andrews, *Sea Shells of the Texas Coast* (Austin, TX: University of Texas Press, 1971).
28   Charles Sassine, Personal Communication. Division of Science and Resources Management, Padre Island National Seashore.
29   Texas Parks and Wildlife. Blue Crab (Callinectes sapidus). Accessed August 25, 2021. https://tpwd.texas.gov/huntwild/wild/species/bluecrab/.

Part 8: Glimpses into a Few Traditions
Chapter 30: Dreaming Yom Kippur
30   C. G. Jung (Author), Aniela Jaffe (Editor), Richard Winston (Translator), Clara Winston (Translator) *Memories, Dreams, and Reflections* Hardcover, May 12, 1963 (New York: Vintage Books, Random House, 1989).
31   Houston International Folkdancers. August 25, 2021. https://www.folkdancers.org/.
32   Alfred J. Kolatch, Chapter 11, "The High Holidays" *The Jewish Book of Why* (New York: Jonathan David Publishers, 1981) 221-245.
33   *Prayer Book and Hymnal* (New York: Episcopal Church, The Church Hymnal Corporation, 1986).

34 Baha'i Reference Library, Writings of Baha'u'lla'h, Tablets of Baha'u'lla'h, Glad Tidings 9. Accessed 8/30/2021, www.Bahai.org.

35 Bill W., *Twelve Steps and Twelve Traditions* (Alcoholics Anonymous Word Services, 1952). Accessed 8/30/2021. https://aa.org.

36 "Atonement." Merriam-Webster.com Dictionary, Merriam-Webster, Accessed August 31, 2021. https://www.merriam-webster.com/dictionary/atonement.

37 Lawrence Van Ypersele (2012), ed. John Horne, *Mourning and Memory, 1919–45. A Companion to World War I*; Wiley, p. 584. (Cited by Wikipedia in World War I.)

38 Tony Judt, *Postwar: A History of Europe Since 1945*, Chapter III: "Rehabilitation" and Chapter IV: "The Impossible Settlement" (New York: Penquin Press, 2005).

39 Ibid.

40 William T. Sherman, Special Field Order #15, January 16, 1865. Accessed August 31, 2021. www.blackpast.org/african-american-history/special-field-orders-no-15/

41 See, for example, Constitutional Rights Foundation, accessed August 31, 2021. https://www.crf-usa.org/brown-v-board-50th-anniversary/reparations-for-slavery-reading.html.

42 Civil Liberties Act of 1988, Public Law 100 383, Statute 102 904. Accessed August 31, 2021. https://uscode.house.gov/statutes/pl/100/383.pdf.

43 Truth and Reconciliation Commission. (South Africa) Accessed August 31, 2021. https://www.justice.gov.za/trc/

Chapter 31: Fasting for Ramadan

44 What Bahai's Believe, "Fasting". Accessed August 31, 2021. https://www.bahai.org/beliefs/life-spirit/devotion/fasting.

Chapter 32: Hearing an Easter Cry

45 *The Aztec World* (New York: Abrams, 2008).

46 Rita Nakashima Brock and Rebecca Ann Parker, *Proverbs of Ashes* (Boston: Beacon Press, 2001).

47 Constitution of the United States, Eighth Amendment, 1787.

48 The Universal Declaration of Human Rights, Article 5, 1948.

49 Geneva Convention. Article 3 "Limiting the Barbarity of War" 1948.

50 The (European) Convention for the Protection of Human Rights and Fundamental Freedoms, Article 3, 1950. Accessed August 31, 2021. https://www.echr.coe.int/Documents/Convention_ENG.pdf.

Part 9: Expanding Horizons
Chapter 33: Travel in Time and Space

51 Women's Sports Foundation. Title IX and the Rise of Female Athletes in America. Accessed August 31, 2021. https://www.womenssportsfoundation.org/education/title-ix-and-the-rise-of-female-athletes-in-america.

About the Author

Nancy C. Russell grew up in Mount Vernon, New York, and then moved with her family to Oklahoma, where she attended the University of Oklahoma and married her first husband. She had a thirty-year career in cancer epidemiology at the University of Texas M. D. Anderson Cancer Center with an interim decade as a massage therapist. Now retired, she lives in Wimberley, Texas.

About the Artist

Jesseca Zollars Smith has always loved creating beautiful things. She has pursued a career as a beauty advisor, an esthetician, and a painter of landscapes, commissioned portraits, and semi-abstract works.

CPSIA information can be obtained
at www.ICGtesting.com
Printed in the USA
JSHW031917151122
33212JS00001B/35